TOY
and MINIATURE
SEWING
MACHINES

An Identification & Value Guide

 **Glenda Thomas**

COLLECTOR BOOKS
A Division of Schroeder Publishing Co., Inc.

The current values in this book should be used only as a guide. They are not intended to set prices, which vary from one section of the country to another. Auction prices as well as dealer prices vary greatly and are affected by condition as well as demand. Neither the Author nor the Publisher assumes responsibility for any losses that might be incurred as a result of consulting this guide.

On the Cover:

Martha Washington, Sotoy manufactured by the Metallograph Corporation. $150.00–$175.00. Liliput by Bremen & Brückman NPA. Schürhoff Original Diana NPA. Singer $175.00–$225.00.

Searching For A Publisher?

We are always looking for knowledgeable people considered to be experts within their fields. If you feel that there is a real need for a book on your collectible subject and have a large comprehensive collection, contact us.

COLLECTOR BOOKS
P.O. Box 3009
Paducah, Kentucky 42002-3009

Cover design by Karen Geary
Book layout by Joyce Cherry

This book is dedicated to my husband, "Red." I could not have written this book without his constant support, encouragement, and enthusiasm.

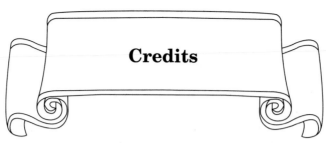

Credits

Most of the photographs were taken by the author, however, many collectors also sent photographs, and others allowed their machines to be photographed. The contributor will be listed under each picture. All photographs taken by others will be marked "photograph courtesy of."

My gratitude goes to all the following for their assistance with this book:

For special contributions: Marjorie Abel for many advertisements with dates and special help in dating Singer toys, Robert Brucato for sharing his research on the Smith & Egge Company and Lindstrom Company, Graham Forsdyke for the condition chart, Maggie Snell for research information from ISMACS News, Georg Reinfelder for the German Dictionary, Toy Treadle article, and machine identifications, and Claire Toschi for the parts diagram and research information as editor of *Toy Stitchers*.

For allowing me to photograph their collections: Glenda Scott, Janice Starkey, and my terrific sister, Wanda Wilson.

For allowing me to photograph their prized machines: Pat Aulds, Cathy Jones, Karen Kohler, Sherry Strange, Pat Wheeler, Kimberly Woeckener, and Fern Wright.

The following spent hours photographing special machines and sending the pictures, measurements, and other information: Marjorie Abel, Judy Arnold, Robert Brucato, Cumberland Model and Toy Museum, Louise Dwortschek, Enesco Corporation, Peggy Foust, Pauline Glidden Toy Museum, Marc Horovitz, Cheryl Landsdown, Clotilde, Joseph and Louisa Llull, Ginny Meinig, Conrad and Jo Ann Overton, Georg Reinfelder, Sewing Machine and Iron Museum in Munich, James and Sandra Seymour, Frank Smith, Maggie Snell, Ivan Steiger, Claire Toschi, VWS, Inc., Harold Warp Pioneer Village Foundation, Joe and Evelyn Watkins, and Estelle Zalkin.

Companies, individuals, libraries, and chambers of commerce that gave assistance are:

Ace Sewing Center—Pat Aulds
American Greeting Corp.
Jean Anderson
Elena Augustinova Anderson
Bernina of America, Inc.
Britains Petite, Ltd.
British Toy & Hobby Assoc.
Brother International Corp.
Catchall—Chris Owen
Chamber of Commerce—Booneville, AR
Clotilde, Inc.
Chamber of Commerce, Jersey City, NJ
CPI Photo Finish, Wichita Falls, TX
Lis Crow
Elna Corp.
Enesco Corp.
Gromes Sewing Center—Richard Gromes
Hallmark Cards, Inc.
Tony Hartl
Terry Holbert—Electra Public Library
Barbara Janssen, Smithsonian Institute
Jaymar Toys Ltd.—Frank Trinca, President

Jersey City Public Library, Jersey City, NJ
Linda Jones
Kemp Public Library—Wichita Falls, TX
Linda Leahy
Mattel, Inc.
John McKelvey
Metro Photo, Wichita Falls, TX
Montgomery Ward, Inc.
Nationmark, Inc.—Carrolton, TX
J. C. Penney Company, Inc.
Pfaff American Sales Corp.
Plainfield Public Library —Plainfield, NJ
Anne Powell, Ltd.
San Francisco Music Box Co.
Sears
Signature—American & Efird, Inc.
The Singer Company
Frank Smith, Antique Sewing Machine Museum
Bonita Tissot
Tomy UK, Ltd.
VWS, Inc.

Many letters were sent to collectors and dealers for help with the price guide, and a very special thank-you goes to all those that replied. Several asked for anonymity, so these won't be listed.

Numerous museums replied to my inquires about their collections and sent valuable information. These will be listed in the Museum chapter.

Also a special thank you to my editor Lisa Stroup for all her advice and help.

The inspiration for this book came from Estelle Zalkin, a very accomplished author of many articles on antique sewing items, and *Zalkin's Handbook of Thimbles & Sewing Implements*. She has been a constant source of information from the book proposal to the finished product. She always ends her articles with:

"A KNOWLEDGEABLE COLLECTOR IS A WISE COLLECTOR."

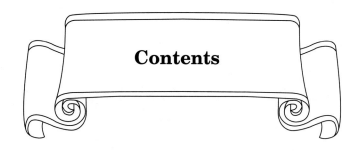

Contents

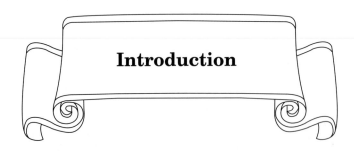

Introduction

Welcome to the excitement and joy of collecting toy and miniature sewing machines. Ladies are not the only ones fascinated by these delightful machines. Some of the most avid collectors are men. Often, collectors are connected with the sewing profession, some are home sewers, others just enjoy antiques, history, or childhood memories. Toy sewing machines, or TSMs as experienced collectors call them, are also appealing for their mechanical ingenuity and beautiful artistic features.

My infatuation with the sewing machine began as a small child while watching my mother sew on an old treadle that had belonged to her mother. I would place my finger on the handwheel as it turned and watch it go around. She scolded me, saying my finger would get caught, but she had great patience since I remember doing this often.

In 1976 my collection began with the tiny miniature sewing machines for doll houses. These took up very little space. Then, I fell in love with the toys, and later added a few of the vintage adult models and other sewing machine memorabilia. Now this has increased to large files of information.

In this writer's opinion, the art of home sewing is gradually losing appeal with the younger generation. Child's play is usually a mimicry of adult behavior using everyday objects that adults use. Many women work outside the home today, and do not sew. From 1900 to the 1960s, women sewed out of necessity, and this is probably why so many different kinds of toy sewing machines were available during those years. The old metal toys were more durable than the lightweight plastic ones manufactured today. Numerous toys are still available to entice a young seamstress into a creative and satisfying profession or hobby. Toys are important teaching aids. If you want to spark an interest for sewing in your child you should purchase the book. *The Purple Kangaroo*, by Bob Benz, an Original Roo Adventure book published by Palmer/Pletch. This has delightful adventures about a purple kangaroo that sews on a sewing machine.

More brands, kinds, variations, and ages of toy sewing machines are available than can be imagined. This book will attempt to show many of these, antique and modern, but won't cover every single one since the spectrum is so vast. A few of the machines shown are very small domestic adult machines that might be mistaken for toys, but these will be identified as adult models.

Some of the very first toy models were round in shape. Near the turn of the century, toy treadles were on the market. The most ornate toy sewing machines were produced from 1900 to the beginning of World War II. These tended to be highly decorative with beautiful gold rococo bases, brilliant flowers, colorful art deco, and folk art designs. Others featured historical people and movie stars. Nursery rhyme and story book characters were depicted, with Little Red Riding Hood on one Casige model.

After World War II, the style changed to contemporary, similar to some of their adult name brand counterparts produced by the major sewing machine companies. Music boxes were added to entice the young seamstress. Department stores and catalog companies put their names on toy sewing machines.

Plastic models of more recent years are fun to collect. These come in a wide variety to tempt the collector. Some feature cartoon characters. The trademarks of Hallmark Cards Inc., American Greeting Cards, and others were used for decoration. A current brand made in China is manufactured in the shape of puppies, ponies, ducks, and kittens. Even the toddler was not overlooked by the toy companies. A rhythmic sound of sewing is heard as the fake needles go up and down on these brilliantly colored toys.

Many people have made contributions to this book. The replies to my letters of inquiry have been fantastic. Museums have been very cooperative. Even the large companies have taken the time to answer and furnish any information they have available. Companies have sold, merged with others, or gone out of business, and very few records have been kept on toy sewing machines. Tracing their history and age is both fascinating and frustrating, since many machines are unmarked. This search makes one feel like a real detective. A great deal of information came from other collectors who have original boxes and instruction sheets with manufacturing information on them. One of the most enjoyable aspects of collecting toy sewing machines has been corresponding with other collectors. Sharing a hobby and trading duplicates and information is part of the fun of collecting.

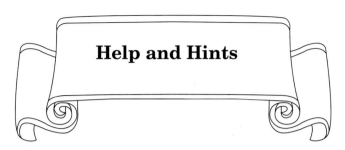

Help and Hints

This book will concentrate mainly on toy sewing machines. A little company history will be sprinkled in, but this book is not intended to give you a history of the invention of the sewing machine — many good books have already been written on that subject. However, this knowledge is very helpful, as many toy sewing machines are counterparts of their adult models. This awareness gives you a firm foundation for identifying and dating the toy.

Dating toy sewing machines is often difficult, as they very seldom have serial numbers, and companies did not keep records. A few instruction sheets and boxes have dates. The company address is often a clue. Beginning in 1943, US Postal Zones were introduced (example New York, 10 New York). The Zone Improvement Plan began July 1, 1963, with zip codes (example New York, New York 11010).

The great World Wars played a big part in the history of the toy sewing machine. After World War I, in England, the imports from Germany were often only marked "Foreign." During World War II, just about all toy production ceased and shifted to defense work, and many companies did not resume toy production after the war. In 1945, Germany was divided into zones by the Americans, British, French, and Soviets. The toy sewing machines were stamped with these zones after World War II. In 1949, Germany became what is commonly known as East Germany and West Germany. "Made in Germany" would indicate pre World War II, and "Made in Western Germany" would indicate post World War II.

Since you can't tell size by a photograph, the machines featured in this book will have measurements. The illustration will show you how the measurements were taken, from the highest to the widest point. Many different collectors measured the machines, and measuring procedures may vary, so consider these measurements approximate, not exact.

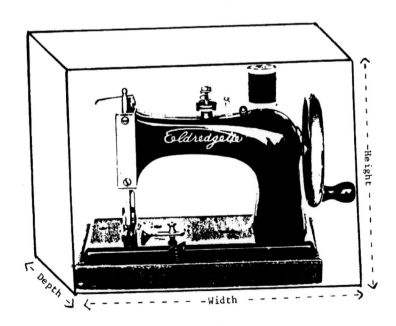

The same question arises again and again: "Is this a toy or adult machine?" Instruction sheets, boxes, and advertisements for a few of the small vintage machines say that it is not a toy but simple enough for a child to operate, small enough to fit in a suitcase for travel, and sews just like the large models. An article in *ISMACS News* calls these machines "Mugwumps," which is a politician setting on the fence with their mug on one side and their whump on the other. This statement "not a toy" was probably an indication of quality. Perhaps, the manufacturer used this ploy to gain sales from both markets. Singer, Elna, Smith and Egge, and Foley and Williams are a few of the companies that made these statements. Most collectors place these in the toy category. Many of the boxes and instructions show a child sewing. This author places all of these in the toy category if the box or advertisement mentions a child. The Singer box is an illustration of the statement, "Not a toy."

Toy sewing machines are a very good investment. Their popularity has increased and values have skyrocked in the last 15 years. In 1976, the purchase price for most models was about five or ten dollars. This is not true today. The quality and age are of prime importance in determining value. Original boxes, instruction sheets, or manuals increase the value. Anyone contemplating collecting this novel toy with only modest capital or limited display space, might consider specializing. There is something for every purse size and individual taste. One lady only collects pink models, others desire the old black cast iron, a certain gentleman seeks treadles, while others just collect one brand.

The value guide of this book has been one of the most time consuming parts to prepare. Many letters and lists of toy sewing machines were sent to dealers and collectors for their input. When the lists were returned, the prices were averaged. If no prices were available for averaging, these are marked NPA (no price available). Prices varied greatly from one section of the country to another, therefore most values will have a high and low. Some photographs came from Europe, but this guide will only reflect USA prices.

Maintain good records for insurance purposes, as these are valuable assets. You should have a good photograph of each one.

Repairing the toys to working condition is not hard, but requires a little mechanical ability, however, spare parts are hard to find. Purchase machines in bad condition for parts. These are usually a bargain price. Restoring the machine's paint, decorations, and metal brightness is another situation. This can be very complicated. If done improperly, the antique value can be ruined. Get expert advise before proceeding. It is a collector's nightmare to find a rare machine that has been repainted.

When trading, selling, or advertising machines, it is an excellent idea for everyone to use the same system. The following condition chart has been formulated by Graham Forsdyke, research editor of *ISMACS News*, the Journal of the International Sewing Machine Collectors' Society. He is very knowledgeable about the restoration and condition of machines, both toy and domestic. He has very generously allowed the use of his chart in this book. The chart was formulated so collectors and dealers can have a better system of determining the condition of the items rather than using the terms: mint, very good, good, or poor.

Condition Chart

10. **Just like the day it left the factory, not a scratch or mark upon it.**

9. **As 10 but with the small, odd scratch or wear mark evident to very close inspections.**

8. **Very good used condition. All paint good, all metal work bright. What the average antique dealer would call "perfect."**

7. **Good condition but rubbing of paint evident and some nickel worn.**

6. **As in 7 but more wear to paint and some surface rust to the bright work.**

5. **The average hard-used, ill-cared-for machine looking for someone to love it.**

4. **Poor condition, chipped enamel, rusty metalwork but acceptable for a collection if a rare machine.**

3. **In need of restoration but a reasonable job for a dedicated enthusiast.**

2. **Total restoration needed to paint and bright metal. It is a brave collector that takes it on.**

1. **Spare parts only and these would be in need of extensive restoration.**

This scale takes no notice of mechanical condition. If something is broken or missing this should be stated, not hidden behind a number.

By: Graham Forsdyke

Parts for Toy Sewing Machines

Claire Toschi, editor of *Toy Stitchers*, has very generously allowed the use of her diagram of toy sewing machine parts. *Toy Stitchers* is a publication dedicated to toy sewing machines. This diagram was originally published in *Toy Stitchers* in December 1990. She drew this sketch for the purpose of showing where parts of the machine are located. It is a mixture of many toy sewing machines. When a term is used to identify a particular part, you can use this diagram as a guide.

1. ....Arm
2. ....Face plate
3. ....Sewing or throat plate
4. ....Stitch regulator
5. ....Spool pin
6. ....Presser bar
7. ....Bed
8. ....Feed dog
9. ....Tension post, disc, spring, and nut
10. ....Eyelet (old toy)
11. ....Seam gauge
12. ....Clamp
13. ....Handwheel
14. ....Driving handle
15. ....Needle

16. ....Presser foot
17. ....Thread eye or guide
18. ....Needle bar
19. ....Modern tension
20. ....On/off switch
21. ....Set screw to hold needle
22. ....Looper
23. ....Base
24. ....Old fashioned tension spring
25. ....Disc
26. ....Top tension nut
27. ....Foot pedal
28. ....Extension table
29. ....Feet
30. ....Slide plate for bobbin

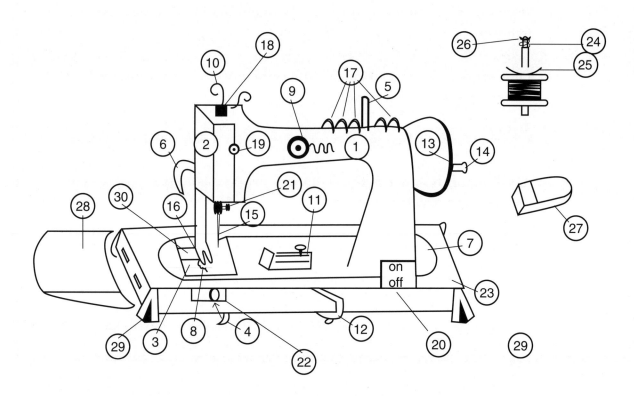

Many toy sewing machines manufactured in Germany have been imported by English speaking countries, and some originally made for Germans have ended up in the hands of American or English collectors. Various instructions sheets were written in the German language, and the toys have German words and abbreviations on them. Georg Reinfelder of Germany has offered the following dictionary to help with the translation. This dictionary could also be used to translate German sewing books and magazines.

English translation of the diacritical German marks, ä, ö, ß and ü – ae, oe ss, and ue.

German	English
Abdeckhaube	cover
Abziehbild	transfer
Anleger	gauge
Bild	picture, photo
Breite	depth
Bügeleisen	iron
Doppelstich	lockstitch
D. R. G. M. Deutsches Reichs Gebrauchsmuster	patent protection
D.R. P. Deutsches Reichs-Patent	Patent
elektrischer Antrieb	electric (battery or house current)
Ersatzteile	parts
Fabrikmarke	trade mark
Faden	thread
Fadenrolle	thread spool
Fadenspanner	tension adjuster
Farben: blau, braun	color: blue, brown,
gelb, grün, rot,	yellow, green, red,
rosa schwarz, weiß	pink, black, white
Feder	spring
Fingerhut	thimble
Freiarm-Maschine	freearm machine
Führung	guide
Fußantrieb	foot driven
Fußschalter	foot pedal switch
Garnrolle	see Fadenrolle
Gebrauchsanleitung	instruction book
Gebrauchsanweisung	instruction for use
Gebrauchsmuster	see D. R. G. M.
gesetzlich, geschützt (ges. gesch.)	protected by law
geschützt	see gesetzlich geschützt
Gestänge	linkage
Gestellnähmaschine	treadle
Gewicht	weight
Greifer	looper or hook
Größe	size
Gummifüße	rubber feet
Gußeisen	cast iron
Handantrieb	hand driven
Handgriff	handle
Handnähmaschine	hand sewing machine
Handrad	hand wheel
Handschalter:ein/aus	switch: on/off
Haube	see Abdeckhaube
Hersteller	manufacturer
Höhe	height
Holzsockel	wooden base
Kettenantrieb	chain driven
Kettenstich	chain stitch
Kindernähmaschine (KN)	toy sewing machine
Koffer	case
Kurbel	see Handrad
Länge	lenght
Lineal	ruler
Loch	hole
Mädchen	girl
Marke	see Fabrikmarke
Mutter	nut
nähen	sew
Nähfuß	foot
Nähkasten	sewing box
Nählicht	lamp at sewing plate
Nähmaschine	sewing machine
Nähmaschinenöl	oil for sewing machine
Nähplatte	sewing plate
Naht	seam
Nadel	needle
Nadelkissen	pincushion
Nadelöhr	eye of the needle
Nadelstange	sewing column
Nadelwechsel	change needle
ölen, Öl	oil,oil
Ölkanne	oil can
Patent, Pat	patent, see D.R.P
Patent angemeldet	patent applied
Preis	price
Puppe	doll
Puppenkleider	clothes for dolls
Puppennähmaschine	miniature for doll houses
Rost	rust
säumen	hem
Sammlung, sammeln	collection,collect
Schachtel	original box
Schalter: ein/aus	switch: on/off
Schere	scissors
Schnellnäher	quick sewer
Schraube	screw
Schraubenklammer	clamp to secure to table
Schraubenzieher	screwdriver
Schublade	drawer
Seide	silk
Sockel	base
Spielzeugnähmaschine	see Kindernähmaschine
Stahlblech	sheet steel
Stich	stitch
Stichplatte	see Nähplatte
Stichverstellung	change stitch length
Stoff	cloth
Teile	see Ersatzteile
Tischnähmaschine	table sewing machine
Tragtasche	carrying case
verchromt	nickel plated
Zahnkranz	spur gear (inside wheel)
Zahnrad	gearwheel
Zeichnung	illustration
Zubehör	accessories, attachments

Toy sewing machines manufactured in Germany delighted small girls as they experienced their first efforts at sewing. Due to the excellent quality, many toys were passed on to later generations, from grandmother, to mother, to child. A few have survived the hard years of playing and are now in the hands of collectors. With this dictionary, you can now speak to your toy sewing machine in its own language. These toys may remember the words spoken at their birthplace in Berlin, Gevelsberg, or Nürnberg. When you speak German words to your toy, maybe you will receive a smile from the handwheel, or the sewing plate will give you a melancholy glance.

Enjoy Kindernähmaschinen-Deutsch!

Georg Reinfelder

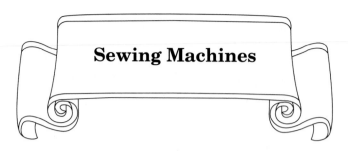

Sewing Machines

All the sewing machines in this chapter are small. The majority of them are toys. A few are portable or miniatures that are often mistaken for toys. Others are considered for adults and children. If the machine was marketed only for adults, this will be noted.

Most of the machines will be listed in alphabetical order by manufacturer. If the manufacturer is unknown, it will be listed by country (example–Made in Japan). Several machines are very well known by their name, and will be listed by name (example–Tourist and Tabitha). The index will be listed by both manufacturer and name.

Artcraft Metal Products, Inc.
West Haven, Connecticut, USA

Plate 1. LITTLE MOTHER, manufactured by Artcraft Metal Products, Inc., came in many colors. Maroon, royal blue, and red are shown in this photograph. The operating mechanism is visible on the back side of this sheet metal machine. Turning the handwheel produces an even chain stitch. A clamp accompanied the toy to fasten it securely to the table. 8"h x 4⅛"d x 8¼"w; c.1940s.

Plate 1A. This dark blue LITTLE MOTHER is shown with the original box. Photograph courtesy of Joe and Evelyn Watkins.

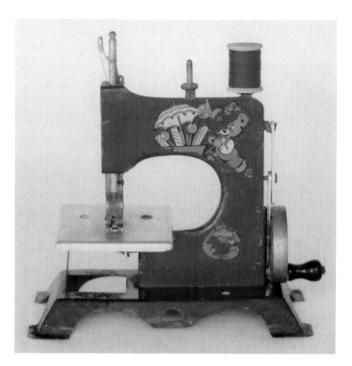

Plate 2. The Artcraft Metal Products emblem, similar in shape to an art pallet, is shown on the lower right hand side. This toy has a teddy bear decal. It sews a chain stitch and came with a table clamp. Most machines of this brand were designed with the handwheel very low. Toy owned by Fern Wright. 8"h x 4⅛"d x 8¼" w; c. 1940s.

Plate 2A. This toy was also available in a variety of colors. Photograph courtesy of Joe and Evelyn Watkins.

Plate 2B. An original carrying case is shown with the "teddy bear" toy. Courtesy of Judy Arnold.

Plate 3. LITTLE LADY by Artcraft is painted shocking pink with clusters of white and yellow flowers. The hand operated machine is made of sheet metal, and the mechanism is visible on the back side. A TOY-O-RAMA catalog of 1955–56 featured a Little Lady Sewing Center complete with carrying case, doll, and fabric for $3.98. 7"h x 4"d x 8" w; c. 1950s.

Plate 3A. The sewing plate on the LITTLE LADY was often painted a different color. Aqua is shown and white was also available. Photograph courtesy of Estelle Zalkin.

Plate 4. The JUNIOR MISS machine has a black baked enamel finish. It is mounted on a sturdy wood base and tilts backward to reveal the chain drive mechanism that produces a chain stitch. A table clamp was furnished. The Montgomery Ward Christmas Catalog of 1946 featured the Junior Miss for $6.95 as a "Deluxe Toy Sewing Machine." 6¼"h x 4"d x 9"w; c. 1940s.

Plate 5. This JUNIOR MISS is a metal toy mounted on a sturdy wood base. The machine tilts backward to reveal a cam drive mechanism that produces a chain stitch. A table clamp was furnished. The Artcraft emblem and "made in West Haven, Connecticut" are on the front. The toy came in a variety of colors as shown in black, red, and navy. 6½"h x 4½"d x 10"w; c. 1940s and 1950s.

Plate 6. The JUNIOR MISS was also available trimmed with a multitude of flowers. 6½"h x 4½"d x 10"w; c. 1940s-1950s.

Baby

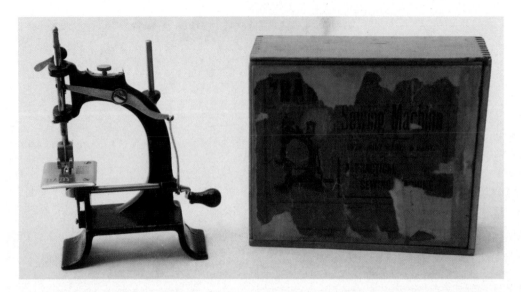

Plate 7. This small cast-iron machine came in a wooden box that says, "Everybody wants a BABY." Montgomery Ward catalogs of 1896, 1897, 1898, featured this machine. The catalog ad says, "A child can operate it successfully and it will do practical sewing for ladies use." The patent finger protector makes it absolutely impossible to get the fingers under the needle, insuring against painful accidents and renders the BABY perfectly safe for children's use. It fastens to an ordinary table or shelf with a clamp, uses regular Wilcox and Gibbs needles, and weighs only two pounds. Photograph courtesy of Ginny Meinig. 6½"h x 2⅛"d x 5¾"w; c. 1890s.

Batchelor & Stenson
New York, New York

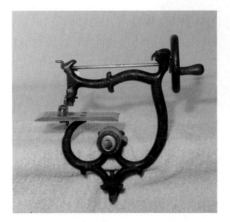

Plate 8. SOEZY is a black clamped style cast-iron toy. The following is stenciled on the sewing plate: "The SOEZY, Batchelor & Stenson, New York, USA, Pat. Nov. 20, 1900, Pat. July 2, 1901, Pat. Jan. 14, 1902." The needle assembly is missing from the machine in the photograph. This toy is considered scarce and very desired by collectors. Do not confuse this toy with Soeze and Sew E-Z. Courtesy of Joseph and Louisa Llull. 7"h x 7"w; c. early 1900s.

Betsy Ross Sewing Machine Corporation
666 Lakeshore Drive
Chicago 11, Illinois USA

Gibraltar Manufacturing Co., Inc.
403 Communipaw Ave.
Jersey City 4, New Jersey USA

"The New Jersey Industrial Directory" shows the last year Gibraltar was in Jersey City was 1965. This directory shows the company in South Plainfield, New Jersey, in 1966, and last recorded there in 1971.

Plate 9. This BETSY ROSS toy sewing machine was manufactured by the Betsy Ross Sewing Machine Corp., 666 Lakeshore Drive, Chicago 11, Illinois. The toy is manually operated and produces a chain stitch. Tiny suction feet hold this heavy die-cast green metal machine securely to the table. The instruction sheet is folded to form a letter with the postmark Chicago, Il., April 49. The letter reads: *I am happy to be at home with you, and to help you learn to sew many beautiful things. Please let mother use me occasionally to run up her curtains and her mending. I know you'll both love to sew and sew now that you have me. You can help Mother and Mother can help you do lots of mending jobs. To make me work easily follow the directions on the other side of this letter. Take a little time and have Mother help you learn, and you will find sewing is so easy and so much fun. Sincerely, Betsy Ross.* 6¼"h x 4½"d x 7¾"w. c.1949.

Plate 10. The new BETSY ROSS miniature sewing machine is a guaranteed product of Gibraltar Manufacturing Co., Inc. At first glance this toy appears to be identical to the preceeding photograph, however, the handwheel on this one is much smaller. The toy is made of heavy die-cast metal with a hammertone green finish. The looper sews a chain stitch as the handwheel is turned clockwise. A September 1954 issue of *Life Magazine* featured a large advertisement of a coloring contest for children that says, "Win 10 big prizes in your neighborhood supermarket." Piggly Wiggly Grocery Store in Electra, Texas, was a neighborhood sponsor. A small girl won this Betsy Ross toy as the prize. Toy owned by Kimberly Jones Woeckener. 6⅜"h x 4¼"d x 8"w; c.1954.

Plate 11. This BETSY ROSS portable electric child's sewing machine fits in a red simulated leather carrying case. The heavy die-cast metal machine has a hammertone green finish and weighs about nine pounds. This model does not have the manufacturer decal on the back, but has Model No. 707 stamped on the front base. Raised lettering on the front says: "Pat. Pending, Made in the USA." The machine sews an even chain stitch, and has stitch and tension regulators. The 1950 Montgomery Ward Christmas Catalog featured this toy on page 104. It sold for $18.95. 8¾"h x 6¼"d x 8½"w; c. 1950.

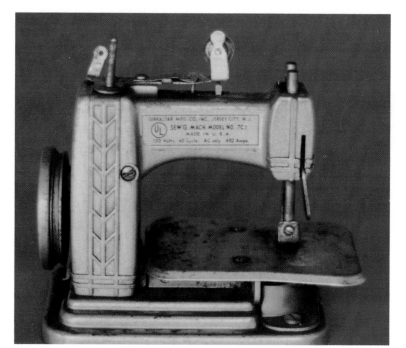

Plate 12. This BETSY ROSS is electric. A decal on the back says it was manufactured by "Gibraltar Mfg. Co., Inc., Jersey City, N.J., Sewing Machine Model #707, Made in USA, 120 volts, 60 cycle, 482 Amps." The base is missing from the machine in the photograph. The price guide will show value if base and case were included. The looper mechanism is the same on this electric model as on the hand operated. A model 707 E was also available with slight variations. Toy from the collection of Wanda Wilson. 6"h x 3¾"d x 6¾"w; c. 1950s.

Bing Werke

Nürnberg, Germany

Trademark – G. B. N. (Gebrüder Bing, Nürnberg)

Well known as a producer of toys, including trains, ships, doll house/apartments, and toy sewing machines. Information furnished by Georg Reinfelder.

Plate 13. BING WERKE produced this heavy cast iron machine with unique gold zig-zag designs. It is stamped "Int. reg. TRADEMARK BAVARIA, D.R.G.M., USA Patent Appl." The mechanism is chain driven. A clamp is used to fasten it securely to the table. The fall and winter 1925-26 Montgomery Ward Catalog featured this Bing machine in the toy section, and the ad says, "This is not a toy, but a machine we recommend for travelers." The Sears and Roebuck Catalog of 1926 also featured this machine, and it sold for $3.47. Photograph courtesy of Georg Reinfelder. 6½"h x 4½"d x 7¾"w; c. 1920s.

Plate 14. Several languages were available on the instruction sheet of this tiny tin type toy made in Bavaria. Note the trademark on the box is a diamond shape with GBN written inside. The sewing plate is nickel-plated. It performs a chain stitch that can be tied off by hand. The instructions state "The sewing machine can also be used as a model in connection with a steam engine or electro motor; for this purpose the handwheel is fitted with a groove." Photograph and information courtesy of Robert Brucato. 4½"h x 2"d x 5"; early 1900s.

Bloomingdale's
New York, New York USA

Plate 15. BLOOMINGDALE'S is written on the upper arm of this two-tone green toy. "Made in Western Germany" is engraved on the sewing plate. It is battery operated with an on/off switch. Photograph courtesy of Joseph and Louisa Llull. 5"h x 7½"w; c. post WWII.

Bremer & Brückmann
Braunschweig, Germany
One of the early producers of adult sewing machines.

Plate 16. Bremer & Brückman manufactured this magnificent cast-iron machine. It was advertised as "best toy sewing machine." It has two names: "LILIPUT" and "COLIBRI." The hummingbird (in German-Colibri) is depicted in the decoration on the base and also on the tinplate cover. One turn of the handwheel produces four stitches. A small tinplate box for sewing accessories is in the base. The handle on the handwheel is made of fine porcelain. Some machines are stamped "Sole Distributor Julius A. Landberger, East Oakland, California" and "Gem." Photograph and information courtesy of Georg Reinfelder. 8½"h x 6¼"d x 11¼"w; c. 1884.

Britains Petite, Ltd.
Chelsea Street, New Basford
Nottingham, England

Plate 17. PETITE is a product of Britains Petite, Ltd. Information was furnished by this company. They purchased tools from Singer (France) in about 1980 or 1981, then this machine was made in Nottingham for many years (final year 1990). It is a lockstitch sewing machine with a sliding torpedo shaped shuttle, moving up and down the bed and containing the bottom spool of thread. Features are: plastic carrying case, attached table clamp, battery operated with foot pedal, and tension regulator. This toy was sold in the J. C. Penney and Montgomery Ward Christmas Catalogs of 1980. 8¾"h x 4¾"d x 10⅛"w; c. 1980s.

Plate 18. This PETITE is a chain stitch machine made for Britains Petite Limited by Mehanotehnika of Yugoslavia. The numbers 0043 E076 and RSO ATTEST Z-77267 appear on the bottom. The plastic toy is hand operated. A small compartment on the back side holds the thread as it does not have a spool pin. A similar item was included in a sewing activity set. This set, which included a sewing machine with case and accessories, was in the 1981 Montgomery Ward Christmas Catalog. Manufacturing information furnished by Britains Petite Limited. 6"h x 4¾"d x 8⅛"w; c.1981 – 1983.

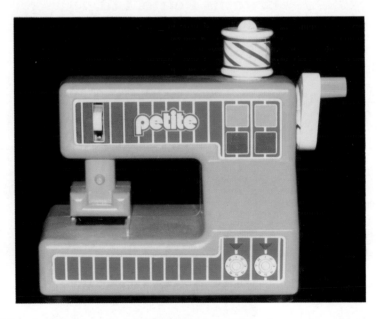

Plate 19. This brilliantly colored PETITE model is not a real sewing machine but was called "Paper Sew." It could sew sheets of paper together by punching a tab through the paper and folding it over. The toy is plastic, sits on rubber suction feet, and is manually operated. Information furnished by Britains Petite Ltd. 8"h x 5"d x 9¼"w; c. 1983 – 1989.

Brother Sewing Machine Mfg. Co., Ltd.

Plate 20. BABY BROTHER was manufactured in Japan for Brother Sewing Machine Mfg. Co., Ltd. A red sticker on the bottom says: "Export Standard JIS S 8001, Labeled by Nippon Sewing Machine Mfg. Co. Ltd." A letter to this author dated July 14, 1992, from Brother International Corp. states that they have no record or printed material about this toy, but indicated it was produced almost 20 years ago. This quality built metal machine has a gray-green metallic finish and a tiny battery operated motor on the back. A small lever engages the motor and a switch on the front turns the motor on, however, the machine makes a nice chain stitch by only turning the handwheel. A clamp fastens it securely to the table. 6½"h x 4"d x 8¼"w; c. 1960s and 1970s.

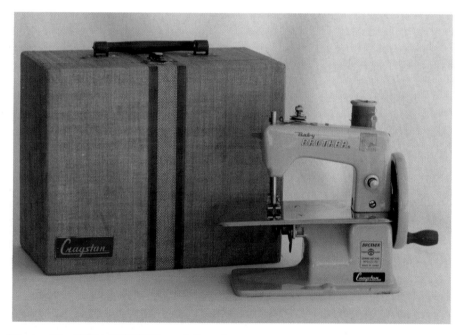

Plate 21. "CRAGSTON" and "made in Japan" is written on this beige BABY BROTHER. The trademark of Brother Sewing Machine Mfg. Co., Ltd. is clearly marked on the front. The instruction sheet shows two addresses: Brother International Corp., 122 West 27th Street, New York 1, New York, and 1058 South Flower Street, Los Angeles 15, California. The postal zone indicates that this machine was sold before 1963. The mechanism and operation is identical to the gray-green machine. Toy from the collection of Glenda Scott. 6½"h x 4"d x 8¼"w; c. 1960s or earlier.

Casige

Carl Sieper of Gevelsberg, Westfalen, Germany, is the manufacturer of this brand. Note the first two letters of his first name, last name, and town spell the brand name. Toy sewing machines were made from 1902 to 1975. The company also manufactured locks and keys. The trademark on the machines is an eagle with outspread wings holding a key. Information courtesy of Georg Reinfelder.

Plate 22. Intricate gold designs enhance this vintage CASIGE MODEL No.3 marked "Made in Germany." Although made of heavy cast iron, a clamp was required to fasten it to the table. The handwheel has an inside spur gear and works with one gear wheel. Variations of this model feature other decor and bases. This machine was considered a functional hand machine suitable for an adult or child. Photograph and information courtesy of Georg Reinfelder. 8"h x 3¾"d x 7¼"w; c. early 1900s.

Plate 23. A multitude of gold flowers adorn this heavy cast-iron CASIGE Model No. 6. The handwheel has an inside spur gear and works with two small gear wheels. The upper body folds back to reveal a small tin-plated box (1½" x 2" x 4½") in the base for storing sewing accessories. No clamp is necessary. The instruction sheet says: "hand sewing machine." Early advertisements refer to it as an adult or child's machine. Photograph and information courtesy of Georg Reinfelder. 9"h x 7"d x 11¼"w; c. pre WWI.

Plate 24. "WESTFALIA-GES-GUESH" is written in gold letters on this elaborate cast-iron machine. This is CASIGE Model No. 7. It was made in Germany. Photograph courtesy of Joe and Evelyn Watkins. 8½" x 5⅛" x 9½"w; early 1900s.

Plate 25. Gold and red geometric designs grace the single sheet metal body of this tiny hand operated CASIGE. A base was probably attached, but is now missing. The Casige Eagle trademark and "Made in Germany" are stamped on the sewing plate. 5"h x 2"d x 5¼"w; c. pre WWII.

Plate 26. Elaborate floral and art deco designs enhance the case of this tiny CASIGE. Gold scrolls, leaves, and green floral designs decorate the toy. Another model was available with identical features but with red flowers. The sheet metal toy is hand operated with an exposed mechanism that sews a chain stitch. "Made in Germany" is stamped on the sewing plate. A 1929 catalog of the National Bellas Hess Co., Inc. offered this set for $1.75. Photograph courtesy of Judy Arnold. Catalog information furnished by Marjorie Abel. 5"h x 2"d x 5"w; c. pre WWII.

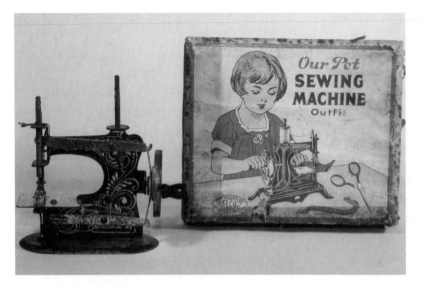

Plate 27. This tiny sheet metal CASIGE with a gold scroll design and green buds is the same as the bottom photograph on the previous page, but with a different box. It came in a paper covered wooden box that has a shelf inside for the machine. The toy is identified as "Our Pet." The label in the left hand corner of the box says "The House of Seco Service." Photograph courtesy of Joe and Evelyn Watkins. 5"h x 2"d x 5"w; c. pre WWII.

Plate 28. This toy is almost identical to the above photograph, but it is mounted on a wood base. Gold scrolls and red flowers decorate the toy on both front and back sides. A table clamp was provided. The tiny sheet metal machine is hand operated and sews a chain stitch. Photograph courtesy of Joe and Evelyn Watkins. 5¾"h x 3⅜"d x 5¾"w; c. pre WWII.

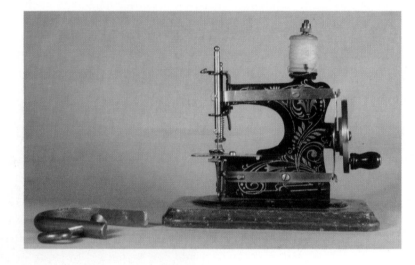

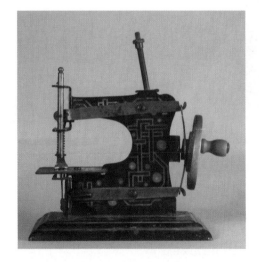

Plate 29. Gold and red geometric designs embellish both the front and back sides of this tiny hand operated CASIGE. It is mounted on a wood base. "Made in Germany" is stamped on the sewing plate. Photograph courtesy of Joe and Evelyn Watkins. 5⅜"h x 2⅞"d x 4⅜"w; c. pre WWII.

Plate 30. The CASIGE trademark and "Made in Germany" are stamped on the sewing plate. Gold scrolls, gold leaves, and red flowers adorn the blue body and base. The sheet metal machine is operated with a cam drive hand-wheel. 7½"h x 3¾"d x 7"; pre WWII.

Plate 31. Part of the embellishments are worn off this model, but the design is very similar to the previous photograph, however the machine is slightly smaller. "Made in Germany" is stamped on the sewing plate. 6¾"h x 3½"d x 7"w; c. pre WWII.

Plate 32. Yellow flowers and green leaves accent this CASIGE model. Flowers appear on the corners of the base also. The Casige trademark and "Made in Germany" are stamped on the sewing plate. Photograph courtesy of Judy Arnold. 7½"h x 4½"d x 8"w; c. pre WWII.

Plate 33. Bright red tulips and gold geometric designs highlight this sheet metal toy made by CASIGE. Tiny tulips also appear on each corner of the base. The Caige trademark and "Made in Germany" are stamped on the sewing plate. A chain stitch is formed by turning the cam drive handwheel. 7"h x 4⅜"d x 8"w; c. pre WWII.

Plate 34. Gold scroll designs and red flowers cover the body and decorate each corner of the base on this CASIGE. A clamp was needed for securing it to the table. The Casige trademark and "Made in Germany" are stamped on the sewing plate. The Montgomery Ward Christmas Catalog of 1934, offered this toy for 98 cents. 7¼"h x 4¼"d x 8"w; c. 1930s.

Plate 35. Magnificent sunflowers highlight this CASIGE toy. Note the beautiful gold scroll design on the base. The operating mechanism is enclosed inside the sheet metal body. It is hand operated and sews a chain stitch. The opening in the base is for the table clamp. The Casige trademark and "Made in Germany" are stamped on the sewing plate. Photograph courtesy of Joe and Evelyn Watkins. 7"h x 4¼"d x 8"w; c. pre WWII.

Plate 36. The CASIGE on the right side of the photograph is identical to the previous photograph, except the machine is painted green. The black machine on the left is slightly different. Note there is no scroll design on the base. The box shown accompanied the black one. Both have the Casige Eagle trademark and "Made in Germany" stamped on the sewing plate. Photograph courtesy of Judy Arnold. 7"h x 4¼"d x 8"w; c. pre WWII.

Plate 37A. Variations of the CASIGE with the story book characters Little Red Riding Hood and the Wolf were available. Black was most common, but they were also painted red and blue. Often identical machines have a different size and design of cam drive handwheel. Sizes of the machines varied slightly. The Wolf and Little Red Riding Hood design appear the same on all machines. These two handwheels show the differences in style and size.

Plate 37. This toy is stamped with the CASIGE trademark and "Made in ermany." The G is missing. The error has been spotted on several machines. The wheel is like the one on the left in the above photograph, however, this same size machine also came with the other handwheel. Little Red Riding Hood and the Wolf are the story book characters. Kresge's 25¢ and $1 Store featured this Casige toy in a 1938 sales brochure and sold it for $1.00. Toy owned by Pat Wheeler. Catalog information furnished by Marjorie Abel. 7¼h x 4½"d x 8"w; c. pre WWII.

Plate 38. Except for the red color, this CASIGE machine is identical to the previous photograph. Even the stamp says "Made in ermany" with the G missing. 7¼"h x 4½"d x 8"w; c. pre WWII.

Plate 39. CASIGE also produced the Little Red Riding Hood and the Wolf toy sewing machine in blue with an identical design. Photograph courtesy of Marjorie Abel. 7½"h x 4⅜"d x 8"w; c. pre WWII.

Plate 40. Note the extra length of the base on this sheet metal toy. It extends almost an inch past the handwheel. The wheel is like the one on the right in the wheel photograph. "Made in Germany" and the Casige trademark are stamped on the sewing plate. 6¾"h x 4½"d x 9"w; c. pre WWII.

Plate 41. CASIGE manufactured this sheet metal toy. Hansel and Gretel are depicted on the front and back side. The Casige trademark and "Made in Germany" are stamped on the sewing plate. Photograph courtesy of Peggy Foust. 7½"h x 4¼"d x 8"w; c. pre WWII.

Plate 42. A colorful Dutch girl and windmill are depicted on the sheet metal body of this hand operated CASIGE. Each corner of the base is also decorated with a Dutch girl's head. "Made in Germany" and the Casige trademark are stamped on the sewing plate. Toy from the collection of Wanda Wilson. 7½" x 4¼"d x 6¾"w; c. pre WWII.

Plate 43. A fascinating box accompanied this small CASIGE toy. Note the girl is sewing on a different model. Many of the early Casige boxes depict various models that were not the same as the toy sewing machine in the box. Beautiful gold and red flowers are displayed on the body and base. The exposed mechanism is operated by hand and sews a chain stitch. "Made in Germany" is stamped on the sewing plate. Photograph courtesy of Joe and Evelyn Watkins. 6"h x 3⅜"d x 6"w; c. pre WWII.

After World War II, Casige toy sewing machines were stamped "Made in Germany-British Zone." Many had the same characteristics, with similar base and body styles, and slight variations in size. Some were richly decorated and others had brilliant colors with the Casige Eagle trademark displayed in gold. A few had tiny legs as the pre World War II models, but most were a more contemporary shape. "British Zone" would indicate that these machines were only made for about four or five years after the war, but a few may have been stamped this same way much later. Several are stamped "Made in Western Germany."

Plate 44. Orange flowers, buds, and green leaves trim this CASIGE. The sheet metal toy is hand operated with an exposed mechanism, and sews a chain stitch. A clamp is used to secure it to the table. The Casige Eagle trademark and "Made in Germany-British Zone" are stamped on the sewing plate. Photograph courtesy of Judy Arnold. 7½"h x 4½"d x 8"w; c. post WWII.

Plate 45. Brilliant red poppies, cornflowers, and wheat are painted on the front and back side of this CASIGE. The trademark and "Made in Germany-British Zone" are stamped on the sewing plate. 7½"h x 4¼"d x 8"w; c. post WWII.

Plate 46. This CASIGE is also decorated with red poppies, blue corn-flowers, and wheat. The base is a contemporary style. The toy is stamped "Made in Germany-British Zone." Photograph courtesy of Judy Arnold. 7½"h x 5"d x 8¾"w; c. post WWII.

Plate 47. The design with the poppies, cornflowers, and wheat is the same on this toy as in the previous photograph, however the machine body is different. Notice that the mechanism is concealed between the sheet metal body. "Made in Germany-British Zone" is stamped on the sewing plate. Photograph courtesy of Clotilde. 7½"h x 5"d 8½"w; c. post WWII.

Plate 48. Whimsical story book characters grace this lovely CASIGE on the front and the back side. This model is eagerly sought by collectors. The Casige trademark and "Made in Germany-British Zone" are stamped on the sewing plate. Number 121 appears on the back side of the base, and the Casige trademark appears on each end of the base. 6"h x 4"d x 6¾"w; c. post WWII.

Plate 49. Thimble, thread, and scissors decorate the front and back side of this tiny sheet metal CASIGE. The Casige Eagle and "Made in Germany-British Zone" are stamped on the sewing plate. A decal that has "SEW-O-MATIC, Trademark" is on the base. 6"h x 4"d x 6⅛"w; c. post WWII.

Plate 50. This tiny sheet metal toy is almost identical to the previous photograph, however, made in USA is stamped on the sewing plate. The base has a slightly different shape. Note the design is reversed and the scissors appear on the left, and on the other machine scissors are on the right. "Sew-O-Matic, Trademark" appears on the base. The photograph of this toy, although made in the USA, is placed with the Casige machines for comparison. Toy from collection of Wanda Wilson. 6¼"h x 4"d x 6¾"w.

Plate 51. "Made in Germany Expressly for Macy Associates" is written on top of the base on the red CASIGE toy with the beige base. Rapid Stitcher is written on the upper arm. The Casige trademark and "Made in Germany-British Zone, GESH M 1470" are stamped on the sewing plate. The solid red toy says "Made Expressly for Macy Associates" on the front of the base. The Casige trademark and "Made in Germany-British Zone, Deutches Patent 935 VII 523" are stamped on the sewing plate. Both machines are metal. Photograph courtesy of Joseph and Louisa Llull. Machine on left: 7"h x9"w; machine on right: 7"h x 8"w; c. post WWII.

Plate 52. Radiant colors and art deco designs enhance the sheet metal body and base. The CASIGE trademark and "Made in Germany-British Zone" are stamped on the sewing plate. The eagle with outstretched wings holding a key is painted in gold on each end of the base. Number 116 is written on the back side. The body is made of a single sheet of metal and the mechanism is exposed. 7½"h x 5"d x 8½"w; c. post WWII.

Plate 53. The art deco decorating technique is also used on this CASIGE. It is made of sheet metal with an enclosed mechanism. The cam drive handwheel turns smoothly to produce a chain stitch. The Casige trademark and "Made in Germany-British Zone" are stamped on the sewing plate. 7¼"h x 5"d x 8½"w; c. post WWII.

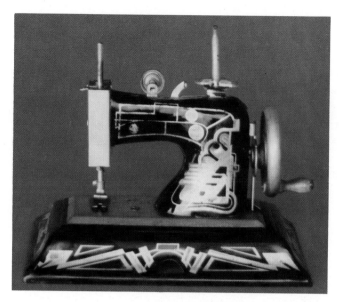

Plate 54. Another variation of the art deco design is painted on the black enameled sheet metal body. Each end of the base has the CASIGE Eagle, and the sewing plate is stamped with the eagle and "Made in Germany-British Zone." Toy from collection of Wanda Wilson. 6½"h x 4½"d x 8"w; c. post WWII.

Plate 55. Gold and red art deco designs are a nice contrast against the black enameled body. The CASIGE Eagle and "Made in Germany-British Zone, GESCH" are stamped on the sewing plate. No. 1015 is written on the front base. Toy from collection of Glenda Scott. 7"h x 4¼"d x 8¼"w; c. post WWII.

Plate 56. Geometric and art deco designs beautify this CASIGE. The trademark and "Made in Germany-British Zone GESCH-M 1470" are stamped on the sewing plate. Toy from the collection of Glenda Scott. 7¼"h x 5"d x 9"w; c. post WWII.

Plate 57. GLORIA is printed in large letters among the art deco designs of this Casige. The Casige trademark and "Made in Germany-British Zone" are stamped on the sewing plate. The sheet metal toy is manually operated. Photograph courtesy of Claire Toschi. 7"h x 4¾"d x 8½"w; c. post WWII.

Plate 58. A green checked case, Butterick pattern, instruction sheet, and sewing accessories accompanied this CASIGE toy. The Eagle trademark appears on the upper arm. "Made in Germany-British Zone" is stamped on the sewing plate. The sheet metal machine is hand operated and painted a bright metallic green. Photograph courtesy of Joe and Evelyn Watkins. 6¼"h x 5"d x 8⅝"w; c. post WWII.

Plate 59. The brilliant red color is a great contrast to the gold script letters LITTLE MODISTE written across the upper arm. The Casige trademark and "Made in Germany-British Zone" are stamped on the sewing plate. The sheet metal machine is hand operated. A Santa's Workshop Catalog, North Pole, New York, titled *Santa's Toy and Gift Catalog* of 1957-58 shows a smaller version of the Little Modiste for $2.95. Catalog information furnished by Marjorie Abel. 6½"h x 5"d x 8½"w; c. post WWII.

Plate 60. Features of the plain metallic green CASIGE are: sheet metal base and body, enclosed mechanism, hand operated, sews a chain stitch, has Casige trademark and "Made in Germany-British Zone" stamped on the sewing plate. 6½"h x 5"d x 8½"w; c. post WWII.

Plate 61. CASIGE with a gold eagle and key appear on the upper arm of this brilliant blue toy manufactured in Germany-British Zone. This model came in many different colors. The working mechanism is concealed in the sheet metal body, and operates smoothly by turning the handwheel to make a chain stitch. 6¼"h x 5"d x 8½"w; c. post WWII.

Plate 62. "Deutsche Patent S 995 VII 528," the CASIGE trademark, and "Made in Germany-British Zone" are stamped on the sewing plate. This brilliant blue toy is a much larger size than most of the similar models. It is made of sheet metal, hand operated, and sews a chain stitch. 7¼"h x 5¼"d x 9¾"w; c. post WWII.

Plate 63. Radiant orchid color and a gold CASIGE Eagle trademark enhance the classical style. The sewing plate is stamped "Made in Germany-British Zone." Other features are: constructed of sheet metal, hand operated, and sews a chain stitch. Photograph courtesy of Judy Arnold. 7½"h x 5"d x 8½"w; c. post WWII.

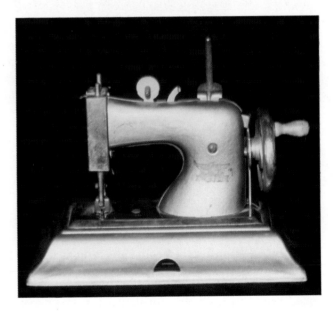

Plate 64. These four sheet metal machines are the same size and style, and identical except for color. The CASIGE trademark and "Made in Germany-British Zone, GESCH. M. 1470" are stamped on the sewing plate. The Casige Eagle also appears on the body in brilliant gold in contrast to the metallic colors: red, blue, green, and beige. 6½"h x 4½"d x 8"w; c. post WWII.

Plate 65. This contemporary style CASIGE had the spool pin on the front. The sheet metal machine is hand operated. "Made in Germany-British Zone" is engraved on the sewing plate. A gold Casige trademark of an eagle with outspread wings is on the upper arm. Photograph courtesy of Joe and Evelyn Watkins. 5⅞"h x 4½"d x 9⅜"w; c. post WW II.

Plate 66. The modernistic style and bright red color of this CASIGE is extremely different from the earlier models produced by this company. The metal toy has a concealed mechanism that sews a chain stitch. A large opening in the base requires a table clamp. "Made in Germany-British Zone" is marked on the sewing plate. Photograph courtesy of Joe and Evelyn Watkins. 7½"h x 5¾"d x 9¾"w; c. post WWII.

Plate 67. CASIGE Model #4050 features modernistic construction. The base is sheet steel and the body is cast aluminum. A chain driven mechanism is hand operated. The battery version is Model #4050 B. Note the opening on the base for a clamp and the Casige trademark on the upper arm. Photograph and information courtesy of Georg Reinfelder. 6½"h x 5½"d 10¼"w; c. 1956.

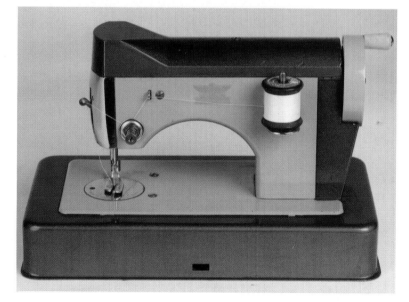

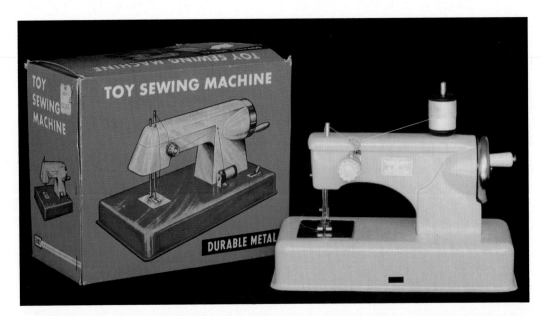

Plate 68. A white and gold decal on the body of this bright yellow toy has CASIGE and the Eagle trademark on it. The durable metal machine is hand operated and sews a chain stitch. "Made in Western Germany" is stamped on the sewing plate. The box says "Manufactured in Germany for S. S. Kresge Company, Detroit, Michigan 48232." This zip code indicates it was distributed in 1963 or later. Original selling price was $2.83. A similar Casige toy appeared in the Montgomery Ward Christmas Catalogs in the 1960s. 6¼"h x 4"d x 7¾"w; c. 1960s.

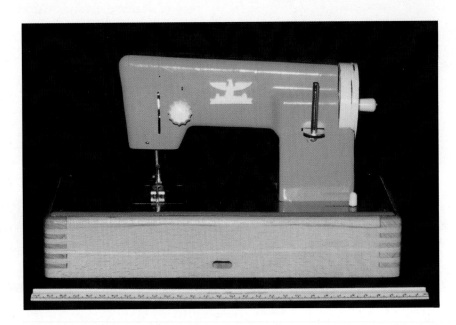

Plate 69. A 12" ruler was placed in front of this toy to show that it is much larger than the other CASIGE models. The two tone blue metal machine is mounted on a wood base. It is battery operated with an on/off switch. The Casige trademark is made of white plastic. Toy from collection of Wanda Wilson. 6½"h x 6"d x 11¼"w; c. post WWII.

Made in China

Plate 70. DIANA was made in China. Features are: made of plastic, battery or hand operated, foot pedal, tension regulator, storage compartment, and sews a chain stitch. Toy from collection of Glenda Scott. 7"h x 4½"d x 9½"w.

Plate 71. This SEWING MACHINE was made in China. It was imported by European Toy Co., Ltd., Item 63261A. Photograph courtesy of Cumberland Toy and Model Museum. 6½"w; c. 1991.

Plate 72. KITTIE model #606, is recommended for ages 8 and over. Features are: made of plastic, battery or hand operated, foot pedal, storage compartment, tension regulator, and sews a chain stitch. It was made in China. Toy from collection of Glenda Scott. 6½"h x 4½"d x 9"w.

Plate 73. SEWnPLAY was made in China. Features are: made of orchid and white plastic, battery or hand operated, foot pedal, tension regulator, storage compartment, and sews a chain stitch. Toy from collection of Janice Starkey. 6¾"h x 4½"d x 9½"w.

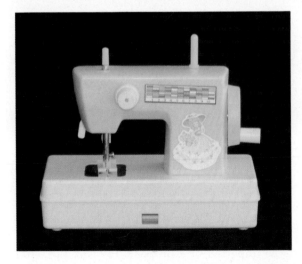

Plate 74. A lovely Victorian doll decorates this small plastic toy. This model is manually operated. Toy from collection of Glenda Scott. 6"h x 3½"d x 7¼"w.

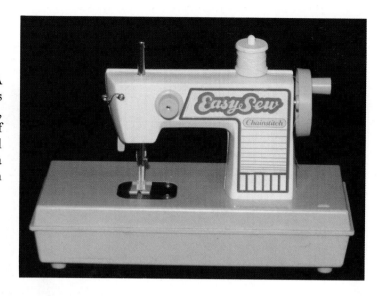

Plate 75. EASY SEW was made in China. A similar model with a storage compartment was shown in the Sears Christmas Catalog of 1991, and sold for $19.99. Features are: made of plastic, hand or battery operated, foot pedal (not shown), tension regulator, and sews a chain stitch. This toy was made in China. 6¾"h x 4½"d x 9¼"w; c. 1990s.

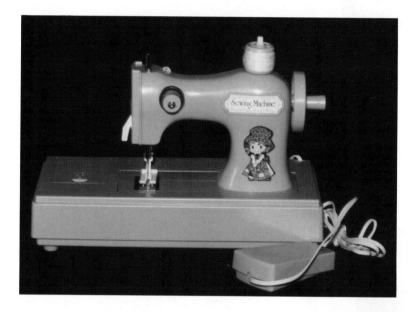

Plate 76. A decal says "Sewing Machine" and an old fashioned girl decorates this toy. "K. D. Mates, Model No. 8508, made in China, and not recommended for ages 5 and under" is written on the box. Features include: made of plastic, hand or battery operated, foot pedal, working light, tension regulator, and sews a chain stitch. 6¾"h x 4½"d x 9¼"w; c. 1990s.

Plate 77. Ribbons and bows decorate this plastic toy that was made in China. Features include: working light, drawer for accessories, hand or battery operated, foot pedal, tension regulator, and sews a chain stitch. 6¾"h x 4½"d x 9¼"w; c. 1990s.

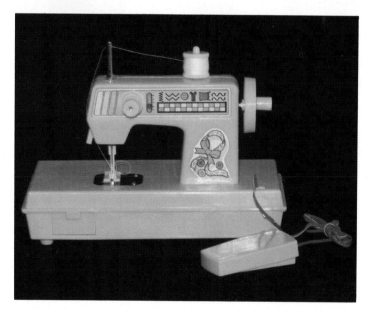

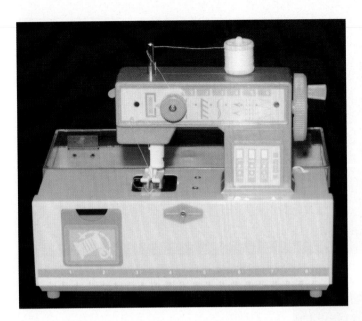

Plate 78. The see through carrying case of this yellow plastic toy transforms into a sewing table. Other features include: hand or battery operated, foot pedal, glowing switch panel, tension regulator, drawer for accessories, ruler on case, and sews a chain stitch. "Happy Bee Toys, No. 63274, made in China, and recommended for ages 4 and up" is written on the box. Open: 7¾h x 7½"d x 8¾"w; closed: 8"h x 3"d x 8¾"w; c.1990s.

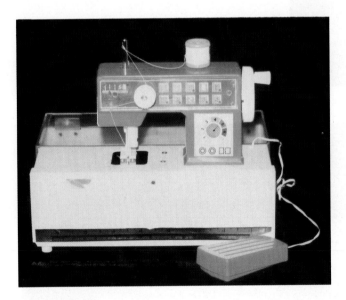
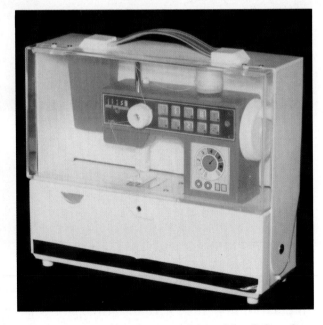

Plate 79. The see through carrying case of this pink plastic toy transforms into a sewing table. Other features include: hand or battery operated, foot pedal, glowing switch panel, tension regulator, drawer for accessories, ruler on case, and sews a chain stitch. The Sears Christmas Catalog of 1992, featured this for $19.99. It was made in China. Open: 7¾"h x 7½"d x 8¾"w; closed: 8"h x 3"d x 8¾"w; c. 1990s.

Plate 80. The EASY SEW LOCK-STITCH, model 8130, is recommended for ages over 8. Dressmaker is written on the front. Features are: hand or battery operated, or A/C adaptable, foot pedal, bobbin and winder, take up lever to pull thread from spool to needle, stitch length and tension regulator. Manufacturer listed on the box is Beng Gang He Ao Rada Manufactory, Beng Gang Bao An Shenzhen, China. Trademark "Kidimates" is shown. Sears Christmas Catalog of 1991 featured this for $29.99. 7½"h x 4¾"d x 10"w; c. 1980s and 1990s.

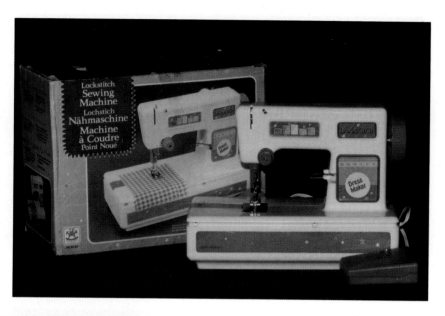

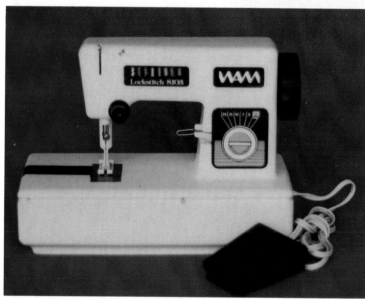

Plate 81. LOCKSTITCH, model 8130, is also a plastic model made in China. The features are identical to the previous photograph. 7½"h x 4¾"d x 10"w; c. 1980s and 1990s.

Plate 82. This plastic LOCKSTITCH was also made in China. The features are identical to the previous photograph.7½"h x 4¾"d x 10"w; c. 1980s and 1990s.

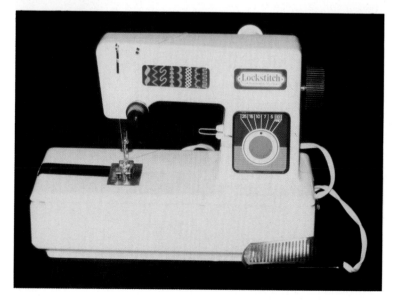

Plate 83. COLORSTITCH has many features: manual or battery operated, A/C adaptable, on/off foot pedal, light and switch, bobbin and winder, spool compartment, tension dial, take up lever, ruler on base, carrying handle, and plastic cover. Kids can control thread color, speed (high or low), and stitch size (large or small.) The toy sews a lockstitch. The instruction sheet says made in China for G. P. T. Products, a Division of Kosbro, Ltd., Elmhurst, Ill. The Sears Christmas Catalog of 1993 featured this toy for $49.99. 8"h x 5"d x 11¼"w; c. 1990s.

Plate 84. This sewing machine has no manufacturing information on the box or machine, although it is very similar to other models made in China. The hand operated plastic toy features a girl holding a bouquet of flowers. 5¾"h x 3½"d x 7"w; c. 1990s.

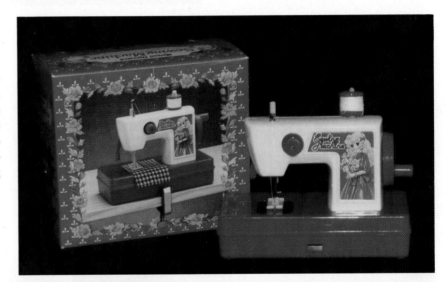

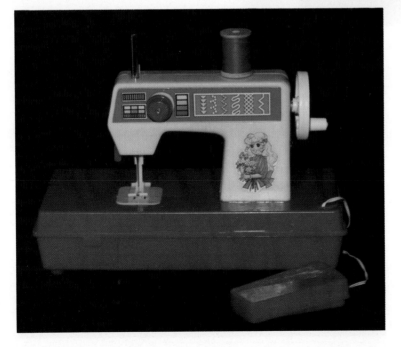

Plate 85. This toy has the same girl with a bouquet of flowers as the previous photograph, however, this is the battery operated version with a foot petal. A tiny drawer is in the base for accessories. "Made in China" is on the bottom. 6½"h x 4¼"d x 9¼"w; c. 1990s.

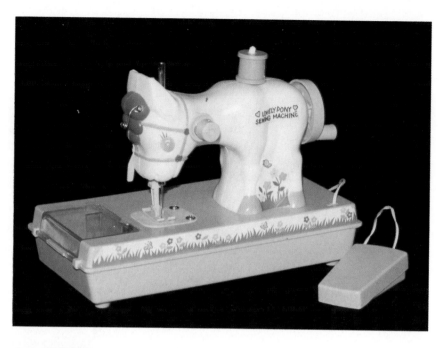

Plate 86. LOVELY PONY SEWING MACHINE is battery operated with a foot pedal. A tiny compartment on the left side holds an extra needle, needle threader, tape measure, and thread. Ngai Keung Metal and Plastic Manufactory, Ltd. manufactured this plastic novelty toy. "Made in China" is marked on the bottom. It sews a chain stitch. 6½"h x 4½"d x 9¼"w; c. 1990s

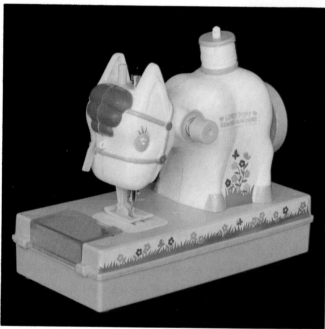

Plate 87. LOVELY PONY, model 500, is a hand operated plastic novelty toy manufactured by Ngai Keung Metal and Plastic Manufactory, Ltd. The trademark NK with a diamond shape around it and "made in China" are on the bottom. A small compartment holds extra accessories. A simple chain stitch is formed by turning the handwheel. 6"h x 3½"d x 7½"w; c. 1990s.

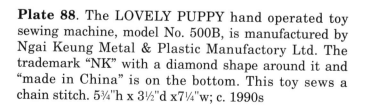

Plate 88. The LOVELY PUPPY hand operated toy sewing machine, model No. 500B, is manufactured by Ngai Keung Metal & Plastic Manufactory Ltd. The trademark "NK" with a diamond shape around it and "made in China" is on the bottom. This toy sews a chain stitch. 5¾"h x 3½"d x7¼"w; c. 1990s

Plate 89. JENNY SEWING MACHINE was manufactured by Ngai Keung Metal and Plastic Manufactory, Ltd. Note the plastic machine says Jenny and the box says Janny. The trademark "NK" with a diamond shape around it and "made in China" are on the bottom. Features are: hand operated, makes a chain stitch, and has a tiny compartment for extra accessories. 5½"h x 3½"d x 7¼"w; c. 1990s.

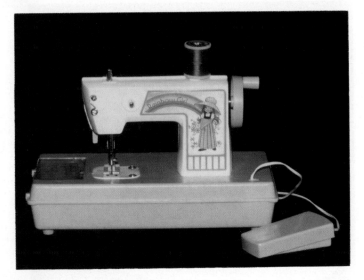

Plate 90. RAINBOW GIRL, manufactured by Ngai Keung Metal & Plastic Manufactory, Ltd. is plastic, battery operated with a foot pedal, and sews a chain stitch. The trademark, a tiny diamond shape with "NK" inside, appears under the bottom. 6½"h x 4½"d x 9¼"w; c. 1990s.

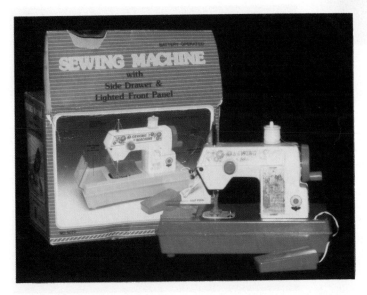

Plate 91. This sewing machine has the diamond shaped trademark "NK" and "made in China" on the bottom. The battery operated toy features a girl on a lighted front panel. It sews a chain stitch. 6¾"h x 4½"d x 9¼"w; c. 1990s.

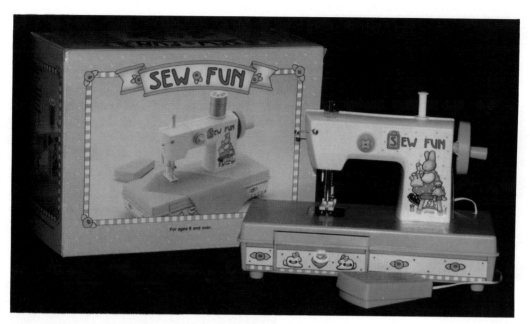

Plate 92. Daisy Kingdom, Inc. 134 NW 8th Street, Portland, Oregon 97209, distributed this plastic child's sewing machine. It was manufactured in China for Wang International, Inc., Memphis, Tennessee. The design is known as the "Honey Bunny collection–Nina 1992". A simple chain stitch is formed by turning the handwheel or using the battery operated foot pedal. A sewing light and drawer for accessories was included on this "Sew-Fun" toy that was recommended for ages 8 and up. 6½"h x 4½"d x 9¼"w; c. 1990s.

Crystal Sewing Machine Industrial Co., Ltd.
Tokyo, Japan

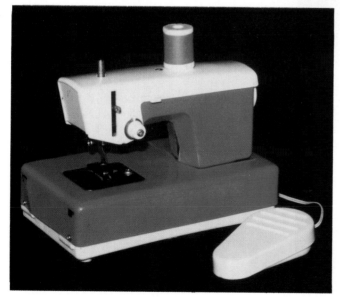

Plate 93. This dark orange and white CRYSTAL toy is made of metal and plastic. Features are: manual or battery operated, foot pedal, tension regulator, and extension table (not shown). The Crystal trademark is shown underneath. 5¼"h x 3½"d x 7½"w.

Plate 94. This light orange and white CRYSTAL toy is made of metal and plastic. Features are: manual or battery operated, foot pedal, on/off switch, tension regulator, and extension table (not shown). The Crystal trademark is shown underneath. 5¼"h x 3½"d x 7½"w.

Plate 95. This dark orange and white CRYSTAL toy is made of metal and decorated with a flower. It is manually operated and has suction feet to hold it securely. The Crystal trademark is shown underneath. 5¼"h x 3½"d x 7½"w.

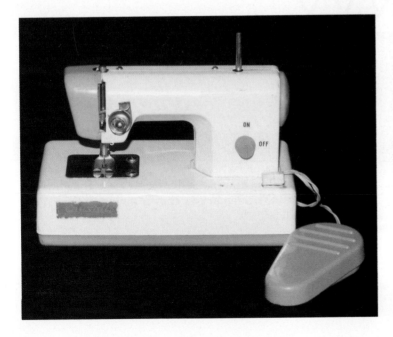

Plate 96. This pink and white CRYSTAL toy is made of metal. Features are: manual or battery operated, foot pedal, on/off switch, and tension regulator. The Crystal trademark is shown underneath and a decal on the front says Crystal. 5¼"h x 3½"d x 7½"w.

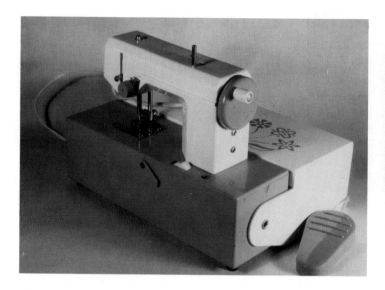

Plate 97. The unique carrying case of this Crystal toy can be transformed into a sewing table. The plastic and metal machine operates by battery with a foot pedal. It was manufactured by Crystal Sewing Machine Co., Ltd. Photograph courtesy of Joe and Evelyn Watkins. Open: 7½"h x 7¼"d x 10"w; closed: 7¾"h x 3¼"d x 10"w.

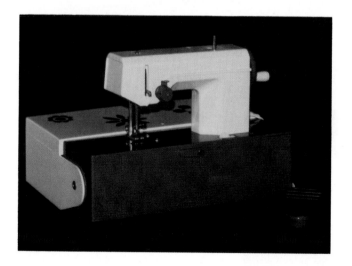

Plate 98. The carrying case of this toy transforms into a sewing table. Features of this CRYSTAL toy are: manual or battery operated, foot pedal, on/off switch, can be used with A/C adapter, tension regulator, and sewing light. The head of the machine is metal and the rest is plastic. Open: 7½"h x 7½"d x 10"w; closed: 7½"h x 3¼"d x 10"w.

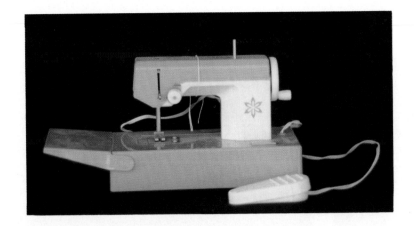

Plate 99. This CRYSTAL toy is manual or battery operated with a foot pedal and extension table (5½" x 3½"). Crystal trademark is underneath. Toy from collection of Janice Starkey. 6¾"h x 5½"d x 8⅝"w.

Plate 100. LITTLE QUEEN is a Crystal toy. It is manual or battery operated with a foot pedal and on/off switch. Toy from collection of Glenda Scott. 5½"h x 3½"d x 6¾"w.

Plate 101. This CRYSTAL has a metal head and plastic base. Features are: battery operated, foot pedal, on/off switch, zig-zag and straight stitch mechanism, storage compartment on front, and plastic case. "USA Patent No. 3633527" and "Japan–Patent Pending" are written on the machine. Patent says Sakae Kasai, Nakakoma-gun, Japan is the inventor and it is dated January 11, 1972, with assignee Crystal Sewing Machine Inc. Co. Ltd., Tokyo, Japan. 8"h x 8½"d x 10"w; c. 1972.

Delta Specialty Co.

858 3rd Street

Milwaukee, Wisconsin

Plate 102. The AMERICAN GIRL (pictured on top of the box) was manufactured by Delta Specialty Company. Instruction sheet says, "Trademark Reg. Design & Lettering Pat. Pend." The other machine (on the right) made by National Sewing Machine Company is shown in the same photograph to point out the similarity of the two machines. The one made by Delta has a light colored wood base, and the base on the National machine is darker and thinner. The upper part of the toys can be tilted backward, revealing a chain drive mechanism that sews a chain stitch. A clamp accompanied the machines. Photograph courtesy of Judy Arnold. 6¼"h x 4"d x 8¾"w; c. 1930s or 1940s.

Dolly Dressmaker

Plate 103. DOLLY DRESSMAKER is a magnificent tin type battery operated toy. The delightful little girl has a red pony tail. She moves as the machine sews. Toy from collection of Glenda Scott. Machine: 6"h x 6"d x 6"w; girl: 8"h.

Durham Industries, Inc.
New York, New York, USA

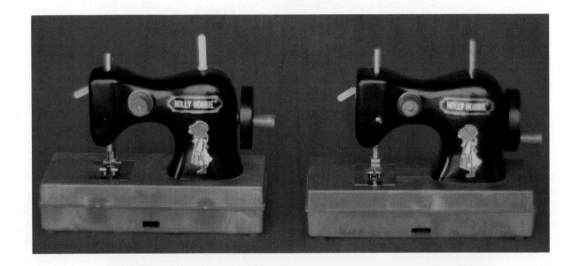

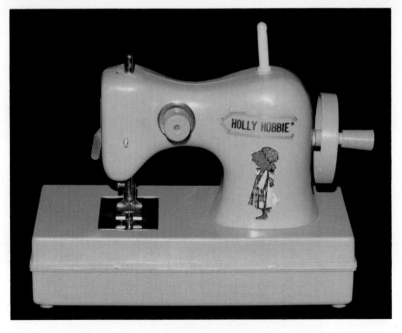

Plate 104. The HOLLY HOBBIE, Model No. 5820, was distributed by Durham Industries, Inc. The plastic toy is manually operated and sews a chain stitch. Holly Hobbie is a trademark of American Greeting Cards, Cleveland, Ohio. The J. C. Penney Christmas Catalog of 1976, featured this toy for $5.77. The presser feet on the two black machines are slightly different. This model was also available in blue. Made in Hong Kong. 6"h x 3½"d x 7⅛"w; c. 1970s.

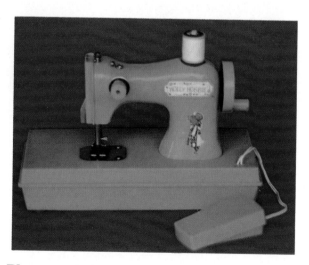

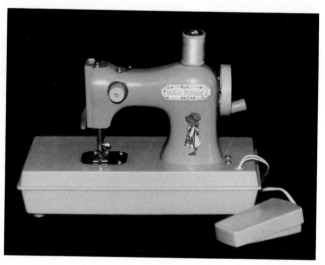

Plate 105. HOLLY HOBBIE, Model No. 5825, is manual or battery operated with a foot pedal and also has a light. Recommended for ages 8 and up. Made in Hong Kong. It is shown in the J. C. Penney Christmas Catalog from 1977 to 1982. This toy was also available in blue and two-tone colors of blue and beige. 7"h x 4½"d x 9¼"w; c. 1970s and 1980s.

Plate 106. The toy sewing machine, HOLLY HOBBIE'S FRIEND HEATHER, is identical to the Holly Hobbie battery operated model No. 5825, except for the decals. Note the difference on the decals in the photograph. One is white, and the girl has a longer dress and a puppy by her feet. Made in Hong Kong. 7"h x 4½"d x 9¼"w; c. 1970s and 1980s.

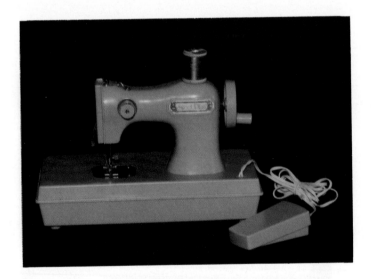 

Plate 107–107A. SWEET PLUM, from Durham Industries, was available in two models. The electric model had a light and foot pedal. The small manually operated one has a plastic presser foot and needle bar. Made in Hong Kong. The color is slightly faded on the small model in the photograph. Large model: 7"h x 4½"d x 9¼"w; small model: 6"h x 3½"d x 7⅛" w; c. 1970s and 1980s.

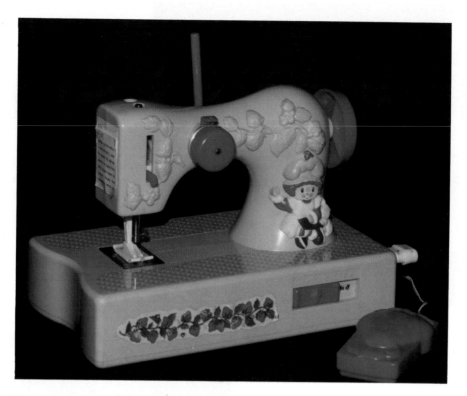

Plate 108. STRAWBERRY SHORTCAKE is a trademark of American Greeting Card Corp. Durham Industries distributed this plastic toy made in Yugoslavia. It has an on /off switch and operates with batteries. The foot pedal is in the shape of a strawberry. 7"h x 4½"d x 8¼"w; c. 1980s.

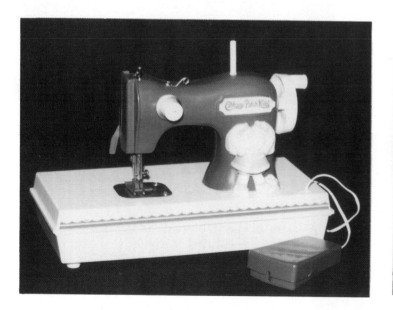

Plate 109–109B. CABBAGE PATCH KIDS is a trademark of and licensed from Original Appalachian Artwork, Inc. The battery operated toy, Model No. 5838, has a foot pedal and light, or can be operated manually. Made in Hong Kong. 7"h x 4½"d x 9¼"w; c. 1980s.

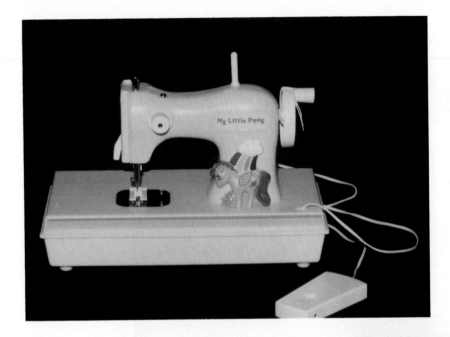

Plate 110. MY LITTLE PONY is a trademark of Hasbro Industries, Inc., 1984, all rights reserved. This Model No. 5844 was made in China and distributed by Durham Industries. It is battery operated with a foot pedal and light. 7"h x 4½"d x 9¼"w; c. 1980s.

Plate 111. RAGGEDY ANN is a registered trademark of Bobbs-Merrill Co., Inc., 1977. This plastic toy, Model No. 5820, was made in Hong Kong and distributed by Durham Industries, Inc. It is manually operated. 6"h x 3½"d x 7"w; c. 1970s.

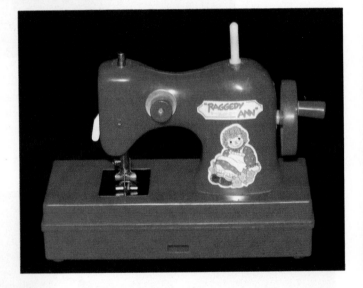

Plate 112. This RAGGEDY ANN toy, Model #401, is featured in the J. C. Penney Christmas Catalog of 1974 and 1975. "Durham Industries, Inc., distributor," is stamped on the back side. Raggedy Ann is a trademark of Bobbs-Merrill Co., Inc. This plastic toy is manually operated. 6"h x 3½"d x 7¼"w; c. 1970s.

Plate 113. MISS DURHAM, style 5810, has a die-cast metal head and plastic base. The toy is manually or battery operated with foot pedal and light and sews a chain stitch. Singer 15 x 1 #11 needles are used. Made in Japan. 7"h x 4½"d x 9¼"w; c. 1970s and 1980s.

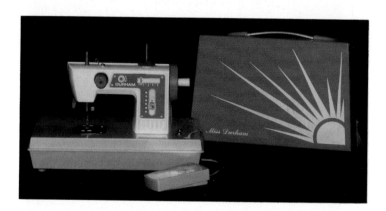
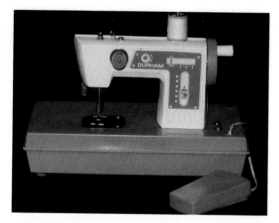

Plate 114-114A. DURHAM was available in several color combinations. The toy has a die-cast metal head and plastic base. It is manually or battery operated with a foot pedal and light and sews a chain stitch. This model was made in Japan and available with a plastic cover. 7"h x 4½"d x 9½"w; c. 1970s and 1980s.

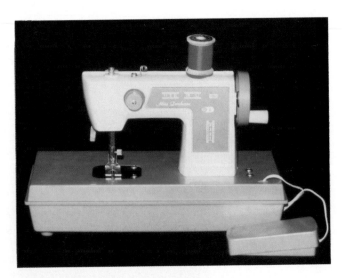

Plate 115. This DURHAM, Model No. 5825, is made of plastic. It is manually or battery operated with a foot pedal and sews a chain stitch. Made in Hong Kong. 7"h x 4½"d x 9¼"w; c. 1970s.

Plate 116. MISS DURHAM, Model No. 5810, is made of plastic. It is manually or battery operated with a foot pedal and sews a chain stitch. Made in Hong Kong. 7"h x 4½"d x 9¼"w; c. 1970s.

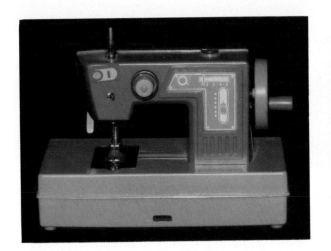

Plate 117–117A. The D trademark of Durham Industries is displayed on the upper arm of this small manually operated plastic toy. Made in Hong Kong. It was available in a combination of colors. 6"h x 3½"d x 7¼"w; c. 1970s and 1980s.

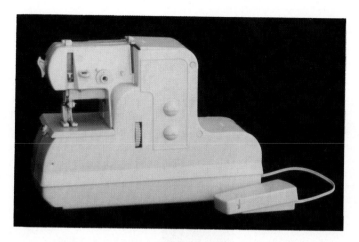

Plate 118. This odd shaped plastic toy was manufactured by Southbury Manufacturing Co., and distributed by Durham Industries, Inc. The top lifts up to reveal the thread spool and the end raises to reveal a storage compartment for accessories. This battery operated toy was available in various colors and combinations including light brown and beige and also orchid. The decal is missing from the machine in the photograph. Toy from collection of Glenda Scott. 6"h x 3"d x 5"w.

Elna, Inc.
Tavaro SA Geneva, Switzerland
&
Eden Prairie, Minnesota USA

Plate 119. THE ELNA JUNIOR is a real free arm sewing machine. It was manufactured at a reduced size at Tavaro SA Geneva, Switzerland. There were about 45,000 Elna Juniors produced between 1956 and 1963. The first model was green and made its debut in 1956. Two others followed: the first was a green base (1956–1958) and the other was beige with a brown base (1958–1963). The Elna Junior could be purchased with or without a music box, and there was a choice of songs. "The Blue Danube Waltz" is the tune on this one. A tag underneath says "Thorens Movement." The instruction booklet states: "The Junior Elna is the baby sister of Elna household sewing machines, which are known the world over. Their queen is known under the name of Elna Supermatic." A clamp was provided to fasten it firmly to the table, and it came in a simulated leather cardboard case. Information furnished by Elna, Inc. 7"h x 4"d x 9¼"w; c. 1956.

Plate 120. The beige ELNA JUNIOR with a brown base was a very good advertisement for the Elna trademark. Features include: metal carrying case, free arm, stitch regulator, and a music box that could be turned on or off with a tiny switch on the front. Different melodies were available. See previous photograph for complete manufacturing information. Photograph courtesy of Georg Reinfelder. 7"h x 4"d x 9¼"w; c. 1958.

Plate 121. The ELNA plastic toy machine is a tiny replica of the adult Elna portable. A Necchi-Elna sales brochure used by Gromes Sewing Center, San Antonio, Texas, in 1958, shows this toy with the following information: "Elna Plastic Toy Machine...tiny, streamlined toy Supermatic...a miniature Elna designed for the pre-school child. Two-tone plastic carrying case can be used as lunch box. Toy from collection of Glenda Scott. $1.95." 6"h x 2½"d x 7"w; c . 1950s.

Plate 121A. The case for the Elna plastic toy machine came in an assortment of colors to please the small child. "IT ACTUALLY SEWS JUST LIKE MOTHER'S" is written on the case. Photograph courtesy of Judy Arnold.

Made in **England**

Plate 122. COMET E.M.C. was made in England. It has a black plastic body and blue metal base with a distinctive design. Photograph courtesy of Judy Arnold. 7½"h x 5½"d x 9¼"w.

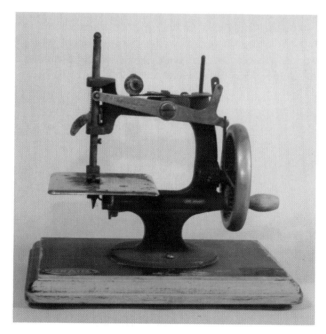

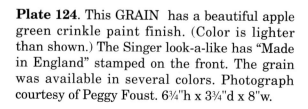

PLATE 123. A small oval plate on the wood base says "GRAIN." The cast-metal machine has a dark hunter green crinkle finish. The design is a copy of the toy Singers from the 1920s and 1930s. It was made in England and was probably marketed as an adult machine, although it is about the size of the toy Singers. Many collectors place it in the toy category. Photograph courtesy of Joe and Evelyn Watkins. 7¾"h x 3¼"d x 8"w.

Plate 124. This GRAIN has a beautiful apple green crinkle paint finish. (Color is lighter than shown.) The Singer look-a-like has "Made in England" stamped on the front. The grain was available in several colors. Photograph courtesy of Peggy Foust. 6¾"h x 3¾"d x 8"w.

Plate 125. This JONES/MECCANO toy was British made, probably by Jones as the guarantee card has to be sent to the Jones Sewing Machine Works at Audenshaw near Manchester. The box is made from white expanded polystyrene with black speckles. The machine was available in a manual or an electric model. Information and photograph courtesy of Cumberland Toy and Model Museum, Cockermouth, Cumbria, England. 10"w; c. 1968.

Plate 126–126A. "PALITOY Sewing Machine– Made in England" is written on the front base. The slate blue metal machine has a unique shape. Photograph courtesy of Peggy Foust. 6¾"h x 4¼"d x 9"w.

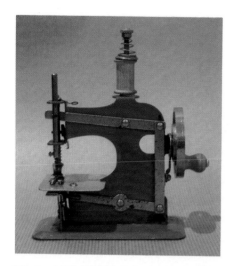

Plate 127. TETRA is typical of the many small machines made in England in the 1950s. This one was manufactured in 1955. Information and photograph courtesy of Cumberland Toy and Model Museum, Cockermouth, Cumbria, England. 4⅛"w; c. 1950s.

Plate 128. This small cast-iron machine has beautiful gilt patterns. It was probably manufactured in England by Newton Wilson, but further information (advertisement, box, or instruction) is needed to verify. Although very small, this is probably an adult machine, as it is too complicated to be a toy. Photograph and information courtesy of Maggie Snell. 5"h x 3½"d x 7"w; c. late 1800s.

The Englewood Co. Consolidated Factories
Chicago, Illinois USA

Plate 129. ENGLEWOOD JUNIOR is made of heavy cast iron and highly decorated. The manufacturer's name is written on the front and also on the tiny gold emblem. "Hand sewing machine" is printed on the front, but the Junior indicates it was probably intended for the young girl. A dome shape wooden cover (not shown) fastens to the wood base. Toy from collection of Wanda Wilson. Base: 8"d x 11⅞"w; machine: 8½"h x 5⅞"d x 11¼"w; c. 1920s.

The Essex Engineering Works
12 Nelson Road, Wanstead
England

Plate 130. The ESSEX is another Singer look-a-like. The machine is highly chromed. It was made in England. This is another machine with the question: "Is this a toy or a small adult machine?" It is about the size of the Singer toys, but may have been marketed as an adult portable. Another model was available with an electric motor. Machine: 6¾"h x 3½"d x 8"w; wood base: 6¼"d x 9¼"w; c. 1940s and 1950s.

Foley & Williams Mfg. Co.

Two addresses are listed on different instruction sheets for this company: Kankakee, Illinois, or 46 E. Jackson Boulevard, Chicago, Illinois. There is a difference of opinion among collectors whether the small machines manufactured by this firm were toys or adult models. They were portrayed in advertising as domestic hand sewing machines or a family sewing machine, or for use while traveling, however several mention kindergartners. An advertisement in the Montgomery Ward Catalog says, "It is practical for light sewing, convenient for ladies while traveling, and for little girls, it is superior to any sewing machine ever offered at the price." Casino's *Little Folks* December 1907, offered one as a prize for selling subscriptions.

Plate 131–131A. The F & W AUTOMATIC is made of iron with steel working parts. Several different floral designs appeared on the machines. Note the design is also on the base. The box shows an original selling price of $5.00. It is operated with a geared wheel that makes four chain stitches with each revolution. The stitch length could be regulated. Wilcox and Gibbs needles were required, and could be purchased for 25 cents per dozen. This machine appeared in the Montgomery Ward Catalogs of 1907 and 1908. Photographs courtesy of Marjorie Abel. 8"h x 4½"d x 9"w; c. early 1900s.

Plate 132. The LITTLE RELIABLE is substantially made with an iron frame, and all wearing parts are of nickel-plated steel. It is ornamented with colored floral patterns. This machine makes a single thread chain stitch and operates with a geared handwheel that makes three stitches with one revolution. The Montgomery Ward Catalogs featured this machine from 1905 to 1908. Their catalog advertisement says, "It is practical for light sewing, convenient for ladies while traveling, and for little girls, it is superior to any sewing machine ever offered at the price." The instruction sheet says, "Manufactured by Foley & Williams Mfg. Co., Kankakee, Illinois." Photograph courtesy of Marjorie Abel. 7¾"h x 6"w; c. early 1900s.

Plate 133. MIDGET was manufactured by F & W Mfg. Co. in Chicago, IL. It was available with several floral patterns. Note this machine has no handwheel, it operates with a cam type crank. The frame is iron and the moving parts are nickel-plated steel. Photograph courtesy of Marjorie Abel. 7¾"h x 5¾"w; c. early 1900s.

Plate 134. LIBERTY is a basic look-a-like to the Midget with slight variations. It has no handwheel and operates with a cam type crank. The frame is iron and the moving parts are nickel-plated steel. A lovely floral pattern decorates the frame. Photograph courtesy of Judy Arnold. 7½"h x 5¾"w; c. early 1900s.

Plate 135. The iron frame of the GEM is adorned with a floral design. Note the difference in the tension mechanism on this machine. It is not automatic. The machine does not have a handwheel, but operates with a cam type crank. A single thread chain stitch is formed. Photograph courtesy of Marjorie Abel. 7½"h x 5¾"w; c. early 1900s. (Another look-a-like to these machines is the PONY, not pictured.)

J. R Foot and Son
101 Gray's Inn Road
London, England

Plate 136. An advertisement for the MATCHLESS says: "This is not a toy, but a genuine sewing machine, that will do domestic work with the same ease and accuracy as one costing 4 guinea, works by hand or treadle, is so simple that a child can use it, and is a most useful present. No home should be without one. Buy no machine till you have seen the Matchless. It is the cheapest and simplest in the world." The firm, J. R. Foot and Son, is the inventor, patentee, manufacturer, and distributor. The machine is made of cast iron. It was only produced a few months and therefore is very rare. Photograph and information courtesy of Maggie Snell. 3¾"h x 2"d x 4½"w; c. 1882.

Made in France

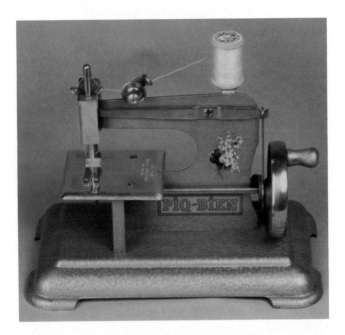

Plate 137. "PIQ-BIEN, MARQUE ET MODELE DEPOSES, MADE IN FRANCE" is stamped on the sewing plate of this practical metal toy. Piq bien means good stitch in English. The toy is decorated with a tiny bouquet of flowers. It sews with an uncomplicated exposed mechanism. Photograph and information courtesy of Georg Reinfelder. 7"h x 4¼"d x 9¾"w; c. post WWII.

Plate 138. This BABY is missing a few parts...the handwheel and the stitching mechanism. Etching on the sewing plate has a double circle with "Paris" printed inside and "RW...JC...LP" printed around the circle. Although this machine is not complete, the value guide will consider this machine in very good condition. Photograph courtesy of Claire Toschi. 7¾"h x 5"d x 8"w.

Plate 139. "BABY " is stamped on the sewing plate. Also on the plate is a double circle with "Paris" printed inside and "RW...JC...LP" printed around the circle. Intricate gold designs decorate the heavy hand operated metal machine. Photograph courtesy of Marjorie Abel. 9½"h x 6½"d x 11¼"w.

Plate 140. "S.M.J. Depose – France" is stamped on the sewing plate. The sheet metal machine is manually operated. Photograph courtesy of Marjorie Abel. 7⅜"h x 3⅞"d x 7"w.

Plate 141. Lovely flowers are painted on the base of this fragile cast-iron machine. It was probably made in France, but more research is needed to find the manufacturer and determine if made as a toy or adult miniature. Photograph and information courtesy of Maggie Snell. 4½"h x 2¾"d x 5¾"w; c. 1870.

Plate 142. This small cast-iron machine is heavily nickel plated and has two spool pins. It was probably made in France, but the manufacturer is unknown. Photograph and information courtesy of Maggie Snell. 5"h x 3"d x 5"w; c. late 1800s.

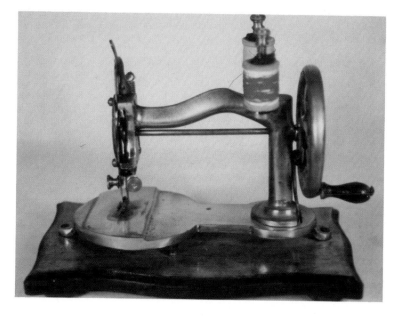

Plate 143. This cast-iron toy was probably made in France, but the manufacturer is unknown. It has an attached table clamp and two spool pins. Photograph and information courtesy of Maggie Snell. 4½"h x 2¾"d x 6"w; c. late 1800s.

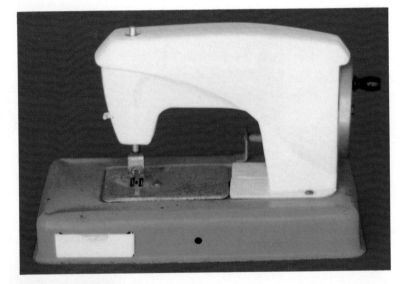

Plate 144. "Made in France" is stamped on the handwheel. The base is metal with a small plastic drawer, the body is plastic, and the toy is operated by hand. 5¾"h x 5"d x 9"w.

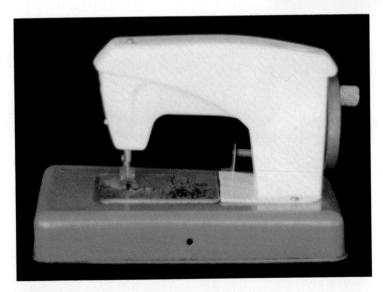

Plate 145. "Made in France" is stamped on the handwheel. The base is metal, the body is plastic, and it is operated by hand. This toy is identical to the previous photograph, except it does not have the tiny drawer in the base. 5¾"h x 5"d x 9"w.

Gateway Engineering company
Chicago 51, Illinois

The Montgomery Ward Christmas Catalogs of 1947 through 1953, offered the Gateway toy sewing machines. Gateway produced several different models. Each Model NP–1 shown has slight variations.

Plate 146. "JUNIOR MODEL NP-1 GATEWAY ENGINEERING COMPANY. Chicago 51, Illinois" is written on the decal on the base. This lightweight steel toy has a red enamel finish. The sewing plate and stamped steel handwheel are painted white. Black suction feet hold the machine secure. 7"h x 4½"d x 8½"w; c. 1940s and 1950s.

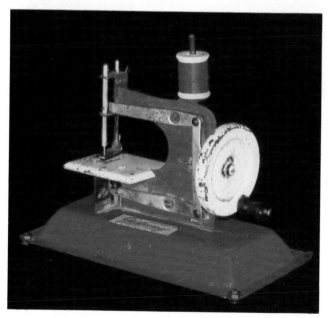 

Plate 147-147A. This GATEWAY JUNIOR MODEL NO. NP-1 is also made of lightweight steel, however it has a reinforced frame on the back side. The enamel finish is a lighter shade of red than the other models. 7"h x 4½"d x 8½"w; c. 1940s and 1950s.

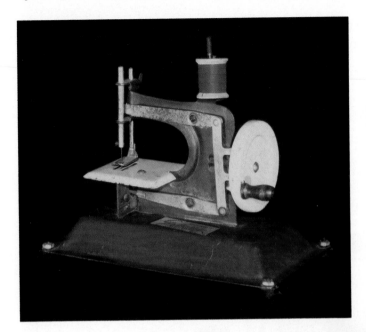

Plate 148. This GATEWAY JUNIOR MODEL NP-1 has a groove added to the inside curve of the frame. 7"h x 4½"d x 8½"w; c.1940s and 1950s.

Plate 149. This GATEWAY model has no decal on the base, however the following is stamped underneath the machine: "Gateway Junior Sewing Machine, NP-1, Gateway Engineering Co., Chicago, Illinois." The handwheel is cast metal with a spoke design. The sewing plate is not painted. 7"h x 4½"d x 8½" w; 1940s and 1950s.

Plate 150. This GATEWAY MODEL NP-1 has a Chinese red crinkle paint finish. The suction feet are missing in this photograph. Toy from collection of Glenda Scott. 7"h x 4½"d x 8½"w; c. 1940s and 1950s.

Plate 151. "Rotar Model NP-8, Gateway Engineering, Chicago 51, IL. Pat. Pend" is written on the decal of this toy. It is sheet metal and manually operated. Photograph courtesy of James and Sandra Seymour. 4¾"h x 3⅛"d x 6¾"w.

Plate 152. The decal on the upper arm of this toy says "GATEWAY ENGINEERING CO., Model NP-49. Use No. 1 Free Rotary Needles." "STITCH MISTRESS" is written on the handwheel. The cast-metal toy is manually operated. 6"h x 4"d x 8"w; c. 1940s and 1950s.

Gem

Plate 153. GEM stands on spider-like legs. A colorful bird is depicted on the flat bed and other gold designs adorn the machine. Note the groove in the handwheel which might indicate it could have been belt driven. Photograph courtesy of Marjorie Abel. 8½"h x 5"d x 9"w.

Genero Machine Works
220 East Pacific Coast Highway
Long Beach 6, California

Plate 154. STITCH MISTRESS is a product of Genero Machine Works. An exposed mechanism performs a chain stitch on this manually operated model. The cast-metal toy is finished with red crinkle paint. Burke-Mayer & Associates, Los Angeles, California, was the national distributor. 6"h x 3¼"d x 7½"w; c. 1940s and 1950s.

Plate 155. STITCH MISTRESS, Model No. 49, is also a Genero product. The cast metal machine is finished with a shiny aqua paint, and the precision built concealed mechanism performs a chain stitch by turning the large handwheel. A clamp was furnished to hold it to the table. This toy was featured in the Montgomery Ward Christmas Catalog of 1949 and 1950. 6"h x 3¾"d x 8"w; c. 1940s and 1950s.

Plate 156. The body style of this STITCH MISTRESS is very similar to the previous photograph, but it has red crinkle paint. This manually operated toy has an enclosed mechanism. A needle guard has been added to the presser foot for safety. The decal on the upper arm is missing from the machine in the photograph. "Stitch Mistress, A Genero Product" is written on the large handwheel. 6"h x 3¾"d x 8"w; c. 1940s and 1950s.

Plate 157. GURLEE is a manually operated metal toy. "Stitch Mistress" is written on the hand wheel. Tiny gold flowers are accented against the dark green metallic paint. Photograph courtesy of Joe and Evelyn Watkins. 7"h x 4"d x 7⅜"w; c. 1940s and 1950s.

Made in Germany

Plate 158. Delicate red flowers trim this mystery machine. "Made in Germany" is the only information on the machine. It came in a red cardboard box with no description. The working mechanism of this quality built machine is chain driven, and shows very high technology. It was distributed by Bayerische Nähmaschinenfabrik A.G. Photograph courtesy of Georg Reinfelder. 5½"h x 4½"d x 7"w.

Plate 159. The clamp on this cast-iron machine is actually part of the machine. It operates with a revolving looper machanism. "Made in Germany" is stamped on the clamp. It was distributed by Bayerische Nähmaschinenfabrik A.G. Photograph courtesy of Robert Brucato. 5½"h x 1⅞"d x 5½"w.

Plate 160. "Made in Germany" is stamped on the sewing plate of this sheet metal machine. At press time, information was received verifying that this is a Casige machine. It is manually operated. Toy from collection of Glenda Scott. 6½"h x 3½"d x 7¼"w.

Plate 161. This black metal machine has tiny gold designs. "Made in Germany" is stamped in gold letters underneath the machine. 7¼"h x 4"d x 6¾"w; c. pre WWII.

Plate 162. BABY (or Federation Baby) is a cast-iron toy manufactured in Germany and distributed in England by Co-operative Wholesale Society. It came with a wood or tin domed cover and was also available on a base with drawers. Photograph and information courtesy of Maggie Snell. 5"h x 3"d x 6½"w; c. 1930s.

Plate 163. DR. HOUG'S BABY is almost identical to a machine called Frieda, which was advertised as a fully-working portable model which could easily be used by children. The machine is black cast iron with gilt decorations and was probably made in Germany. It has been seen with a lunch type tin box with domed hinged lid in either beige or black with filigree patterns. Photograph and information courtesy of Maggie Snell. 5"h x 3½"d x 7"w; c. 1880s.

Plate 164. FLORA (very similar to Dr. Houg's Baby) is a small black cast-iron machine with gilt decorations. This machine is a fully-working portable model which can easily be used by children. It was probably made in Germany and has been seen with a lunch type tin box with domed hinged lid in either beige or black with filigree patterns. Photograph and information courtesy of Maggie Snell. 5"h x 3½"d x 7"w; c. 1880s.

Hassenfeld Bros., Inc.
Playskool – A Hasbro Company
Hasbro Industries, Inc.

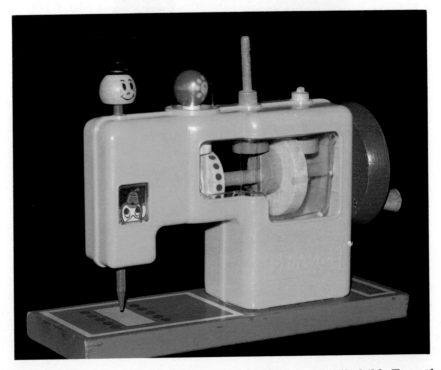

Plate 165. PLAYSKOOL is a "see inside" toy made to delight any small child. Turn the handwheel, and a peek-a-boo monkey goes up and down in the window. As the fake needle moves, the little man on top bobs up and down. Wood spindles and gears turn and the ball swirls inside the see-through dome. Two twirling spools are missing from the toy in the photograph. As the mechanism turns, the machine makes a very loud noise. This colorful toy is made of plastic with a wood base, handwheel, and parts. The J. C Penney Christmas Catalog of 1966, featured this toy for $2.99. 8"h x 3½"d x 10¼"w; c. 1960s.

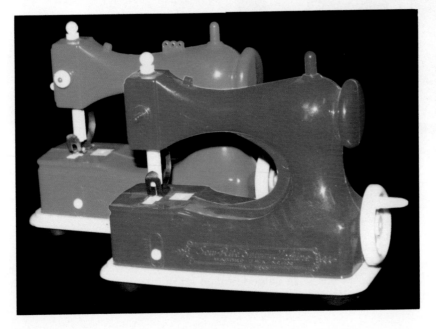

Plate 166. "SEW-RITE SEWING MACHINE-HASBRO-USA-NO. 1500-Pat. Pending" is printed on the front of this toy. The machine is all plastic except for the rubber suction feet and the metal presser foot that is designed to protect small fingers from the needle. Hassenfeld Bros., Inc., Pawtucket, R.I. USA, is the manufacturer. Their trademark is Hasbro, Inc. Several colors are available including black. 5½"h x 2½"d x 7¼"w; c. 1950s.

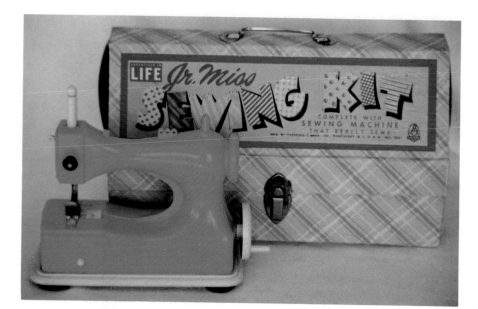

Plate 167. The SEW-RITE toy sewing machine was also available in various "Jr. Miss Sewing Kits." This model is No. 1541. Photograph courtesy of Judy Arnold.

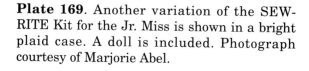

Plate 168. ALICE IN WONDERLAND with all the characters (copyright of Walt Disney Productions) is the theme on this Sew-Rite Jr. Miss Kit, also by Hasbro, Inc.

Plate 169. Another variation of the SEW-RITE Kit for the Jr. Miss is shown in a bright plaid case. A doll is included. Photograph courtesy of Marjorie Abel.

Plate170. SEW EASY was designed for the very young, and sews without needles, batteries, or electricity. Yarn is used to make designs on reusable sewing foam. A tiny storage compartment is on the front. The handwheel makes a rhythmic sewing noise as it is turned. The mechanism operates by depressing the large spool bar on top instead of turning the handwheel. "Hasbro, Paw. RI USA, 1980 Pat. Pend." is stamped on the bottom. This machine has the trademark HASBRO PRESCHOOL on the back. Another identical model has the trademark ROMPER ROOM on the back. The Montgomery Ward Christmas Catalogs of 1980, 1981, and 1982, offered this toy. 9½"h x 5"d x 10"w; c. 1980s.

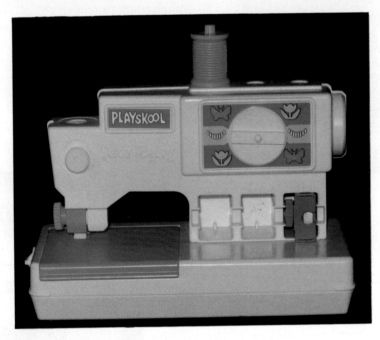

Plate 171. PLAYSKOOL SEW EASY is a pretend sewing machine that uses colorful markers to make designs on fabric and paper. Marker ink washes clean. "1989 Playskool, Inc. Pawtucket, RI. 02862, all rights reserved" is printed on the bottom. The J. C. Penney Christmas Catalog of 1991, offered this toy for $19.99. It was made in the USA, except for motor gearbox, which was imported from China, and markers which were imported from Italy. Recommended for ages 4 and up. 9¼"h x 5½"d x 11¼"w; c. 1980s and 1990s.

The Hoge Mfg. Co., Inc.

Plate 172. This toy has a bright shiny red body with a decal that says: "No. 325 -Popular Model-LITTLE PRINCESS SEWING MACHINE- The Hoge Mfg. Co., Inc., NY, NY USA." The machine is all metal. The Spiegel Catalog of 1937, featured a toy with the same markings and colors. Toy from collection of Glenda Scott. 7"h x 4¼"d x 8¾"w; c.1930s.

Plate 173. This toy has no identifying marks indicating the manufacturer, but this author thinks it is probably a Hoge. Note the base, sewing plate, and operating mechanism are identical to the previous photograph which was probably this model with a fancy cover. The gear driven handwheel is solid metal without spokes. It has a metal eye underneath for the table clamp. 6½"h x 4¼"d x 8¼"w; c. 1920s and 1930s.

Plate 174. This model is a Hoge with an enclosed mechanism. A metal eye is underneath for the table clamp. The toy is made of sheet metal. 6½"h x 4½"d x 8¼"w; c. 1920s and 1930s.

Plate 175. No identifying marks are on this toy. A collector has identified this as a Hoge, however this author has no box or instruction sheet to properly identify. It is chain driven and manually operated. 7"h x 4"d x 7¼"w.

Made in Hong Kong

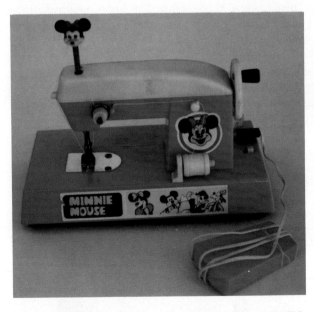

Plate 177. FRANKONIA "LITTLE PRINCESS" is a manually operated plastic toy made in Hong Kong. The F in Frankonia is in the shape of a seal with a ball on its nose. 5"h x 3½"d x 8"w.

Plate 176. This pink and cream colored "MINNIE MOUSE" toy would delight any little girl. The decals across the front depict Walt Disney characters. It is manual or battery operated with a foot pedal that has an on/off button. Made in Hong Kong. Photograph courtesy of Claire Toschi. 6¾"h x 4½"d x 8¾"w.

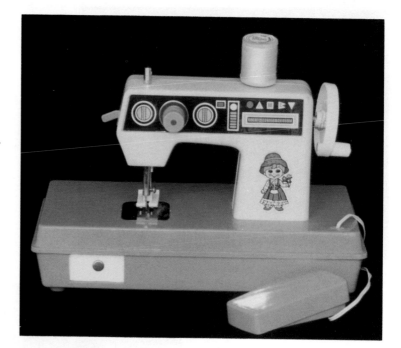

Plate 178. "Item #1822" and "Made in Hong Kong" are stamped on the bottom of this plastic toy. Features are: manual or battery operated, foot pedal, light, tension regulator, and small drawer for accessories. 7"h x 4½"d x 9¼"w.

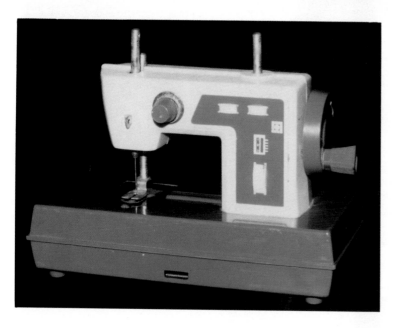

Plate 179. Unitoys Co., Ltd. distributed this plastic toy. It is hand operated and sews a chain stitch. Made in Hong Kong. 5½"h x 3½"d x 7½"w.

Plate 180. Unitoys Co., Ltd. distributed these colorful purple and white plastic toys. They are hand operated and sew a chain stitch. One toy says UNIVERSAL and the other says MISS UNIVERSAL. The handwheel on one has been replaced. They should both have purple handwheels. Made in Hong Kong. 5½" h x 3½"d x 7½"w.

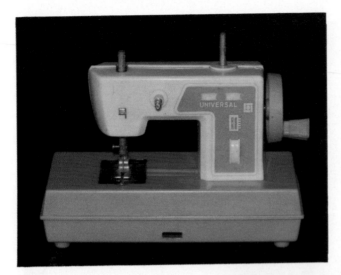

Plate 181. Unitoys Co., Ltd. distributed this orange and white plastic toy. UNIVERSAL is written on the front. It is manually operated. Made in Hong Kong. 5½"h x 3½"d x 7½"w.

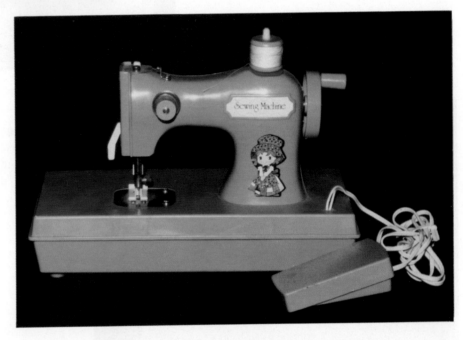

Plate 182. "Item #1085" and "Made in Hong Kong" are stamped on the bottom of this blue plastic toy. Features are: manual or battery operated, foot pedal, and light. A decal on the front says "Sewing Machine." 7"h x 4½"d x 9¼"w.

Plate 183. This blue plastic toy sewing machine is battery operated with a foot pedal. Made in Hong Kong. Toy from collection of Wanda Wilson. 6½"h x 4¼"d x 9¼"w.

Husqvarna
VWS, Inc.

Husqvqarna (Viking) opened its doors for business in 1689, and began manufacturing sewing machines in 1872. They celebrated their 300th anniversary in 1989. Viking and White Sewing Machine companies merged in approximately 1986, becoming VWS, Inc.

Plate 184. Husqvarna (Viking) is a toy replica of the Husqvara 1100 adult sewing machine. It was manufactured by Martin Fuchs Co., in Hong Kong. A powerful motor, hand or foot control, adjustable thread tension, and working light were featured on this item No. 9305. Recommended for ages 3 and up. Photograph and information furnished by VWS, Inc. 9½"h x 6½"d x 12"w; c. 1990.

IDEAL

Plate 185. This IDEAL bears a British patent no. 30, 264. The all steel machine is mounted on a wooden base. It has a walking foot. A tin hood fits over the machine and hooks on the base. The trademark emblem on the hood is a red circle with Ideal written inside and has a gold lion on top. Photograph and information courtesy of Ginny Meinig. 5½"h x 5⅛"d x 8⅞"w; with hood on: 6½"h x 5½"d x 10"w.

Made in Italy

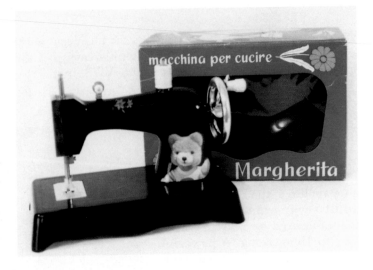

Plate 186. MARGHERITA is a manually operated toy. The adorable teddy bear stands out in contrast to the dark blue machine. It is made in Padova, Italy by C/G Caccaro Grocattole. Photograph courtesy of Claire Toschi. 6¾"h x 4½"d x 9½"w; c. 1983.

Made in Japan

Plate 187. An attached plate on the upper arm of this heavy metal machine says "CORNET." The smaller plate on the body says, "Deluxe Sewing Machine, Made in Japan." A white rabbit with a circle around it appears on the top of the base. Photograph courtesy of Claire Toschi. 6"h x 3¾"d x 9"w.

Plate 188. "ALL, trademark, made in Japan" is written on this machine and the wooden cover. It is very similar to the 1920s style Singer toy sewing machine except the sewing plate is larger (3½" x 3½"). The wooden top fits over the machine and snaps on. Photograph courtesy of Ginny Meinig. Wood base: 6"d x 9⅞w.

Plate 189. DIATO DENKO is a heavy cast-iron toy sewing machine that resembles the 1910 Singer. It is mounted on a sturdy wooden chest that has a drawer all the way across (6" x 10"). An angular wooden bonnet fits over the top. The label on the toy reads: "Diato Sewing Machine—DM No. 1–Diato Denko Co. Ltd.–Fuyono Kamisoto–Murakaminmizuuch–gun–Nagano Prefecture." Japanese characters are written on the bottom of the chest. Photograph courtesy of Joe and Evelyn Watkins. 7⅜"h x 4⅛"d x 8¼"w.

Plate 190–190A. PRINCESS has a round circular emblem on the machine with a crown in the center and says "MADE IN JAPAN." The original wooden base was missing, and this one has been handmade. "PRINCESS" is written on the back of the arm and also in the center of the base of the machine and surrounded by intriguing leaf designs. The heavy machine is belt driven. Photograph courtesy of Robert Brucato. 5¾"h x 3⅝"d x 8¾"w.

Plate 191. This metal machine is belt driven and mounted on an original wooden base. "ROMANCE" is written on the upper arm. Beautiful red roses surround the word Romance on the top of the base. A small plate is attached to the body that says "Deluxe Romance, Yazawa Co., Made in Japan." This was distributed by a National Toy Importers of Los Angeles. Photograph courtesy of Claire Toschi. 6¾"h x 4¼"d x 7¾"w.

Plate 192. This ROMANCE machine is made of metal and belt driven. The original base was missing and has been replaced with a handmade one. The original base should have Romance written across the front and contained a small compartment for accessories. Beautiful red roses surround the word Romance on top of the base. Made in Japan. Machine only: 5"h x 3½"d x 8½"w.

Plate 193. This ROMANCE is also mounted on a wooden base. The toy is metal with a plastic handwheel and is manual or battery operated with an on/off switch. 6¼"h x 4⅛"d x 6⅞"w.

Plate 194. The design on this LIT-TLE SISTER toy sewing machine is five little girls holding hands in a circle around a tree. The instruction sheet says L. H. & C. Inc., New York is the sole distributor. This machine was made in Japan as indicated on the box. The toy sews a chain stitch and requires a table clamp. Photograph courtesy of Judy Arnold. 8¾"h x 5"d x 9"w.

Plate 195. This KRAEMER toy is battery operated with a foot pedal, and sews a chain stitch. The machine folds down to fit in a wood case that is covered with simulated leather. The spool pin is inserted after the case is opened, so this model is often missing the spool pin. This particular toy was received as a Christmas gift in 1962. Toy owned by Karen Kohler. 5"h x 3½"d x 6¾"w; with case closed: 6½" x 7½"; c. 1950s and 1960s.

Plate 196. "ELECTRIC KRAE-MER-LITTLE MODISTE-JAPAN" is written on the front of this toy. The metal machine is manually or battery operated with a foot pedal. The wood case is covered with simulated leather and has a carrying handle. Note that the spool pin folds down on this model before putting the machine in the case. 5"h x 3½"d x 6¾"w; case closed: 6½" x 7½"; c. 1950s and 1960s.

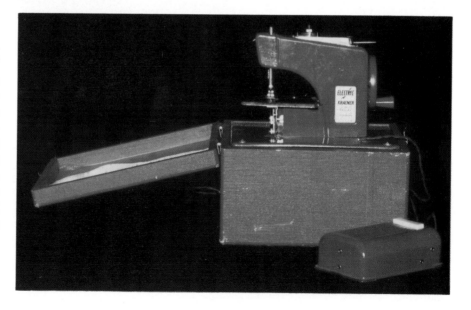

Plate 197. "ELECTRIC–LITTLE MODISTE–JAPAN" is written on the front of this toy. The metal machine is manually or battery operated with a foot pedal. The wood and cardboard case is covered with simulated leather and has a carrying handle. The spool pin also folds down on this model before putting the machine in the case. 5"h x 3½"d x 6¾"w; case closed: 6½" x 7½" c. 1950s and 1960s.

Plate 198. "ELECTRIC–LITTLE MODISTE–JAPAN" is written on the front of this toy. It is mounted on a wood base. The instruction sheet states that it was distributed by W.K. & Co., New York. Features are: manual or battery operated with on/off switch, light with on/off switch, tension regulator, and sews a chain stitch. A sales brochure for Oklahoma Tire & Supply of November 1957, offered this toy for $11.98. Brochure was furnished by Marjorie Abel. 6½"h x 4"d x 7"w; c. 1950s and 1960s.

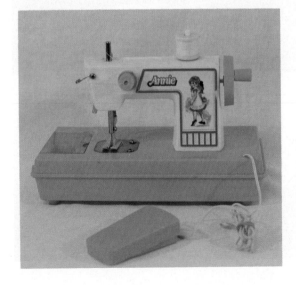

Plate 199. ANNIE is made in Japan. The plastic battery operated toy utilizes a foot pedal. It has a small storage compartment for sewing accessories. Photograph courtesy of Claire Toschi. 6"h x 4½"d x 8¾"w; c. 1989.

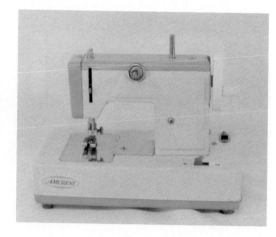

Plate 200. AMCREST is a metal toy made in Japan. This is a battery operated machine with a sewing light. A foot pedal (not shown) plugs into the base. Photograph courtesy of Claire Toscshi. 5"h x 3¾"d x 7"w.

Plate 201. OLYMPIA is a manual or battery operated toy with a foot pedal (not shown) and an on/off switch. The metal toy was made in Japan. 5½"h x 4"d x 7"w.

Plate 202. The metal toy sewing machine has the following features: manual or battery operated with foot pedal (not shown), on/off switch, extension table (not shown), light, tension regulator, and sews a chain stitch. Made in Japan. 5½"h x 4"d x 7"w.

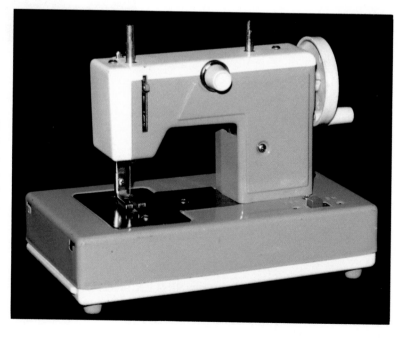

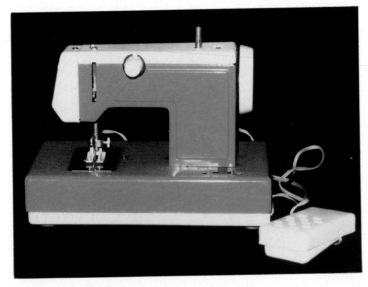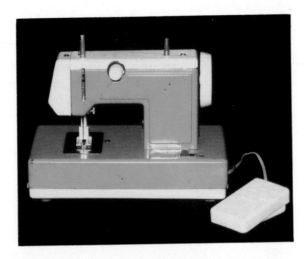

Plate 203 and 203A. This metal toy sewing machine was available in several colors. Features are: manual or battery operated with foot pedal, on/off switch, extension table (not shown), light, tension regulator, and sews a chain stitch. Made in Japan. 5½"h x 4"d x 7"w.

Plate 204. The colorful portable electric Sewing Machine ZIG-ZAG was shown in the J. C. Penney Christmas Catalog of 1973, and sold for $23.98. It operates on 110-120 volt AC, sews a chain stitch or decorative zig-zag chain stitch, has adjustable tension control, foot pedal with on/off switch, light, and snap on plastic carrying case. The head is made of rugged die-cast metal and has metal and nylon gears. Made in Japan. 8"h x 5½"d x 11"w; c. 1970s.

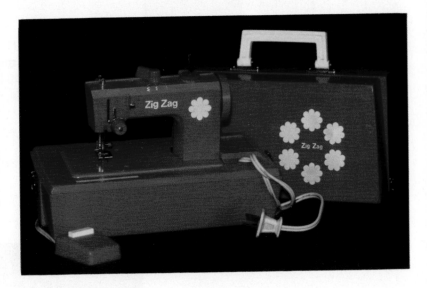

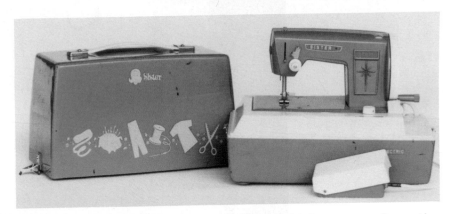

Plate 205. This SISTER electric (A/C 110 volt) has a very decorative plastic cover with handle. Other features are: switch for motor, foot pedal, and light. "Model 25 and Made in Japan" are written on the bottom. 8½"h x 5½"d x 11"w.

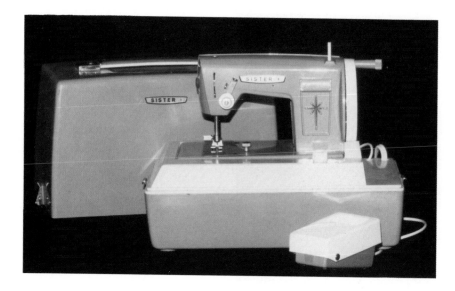

Plate 206. This SISTER toy machine is electric (A/C 110). "Model No. 25" and "Made in Japan" are written on the bottom. Other features are: switch for motor and light, foot pedal, and plastic cover. 8½"h x 5½"d x 11"w.

Jaymar Toys, Ltd.
Rochester, New York

In 1920 Louis Marx financed a toy company for his father Jacob Marx. The name Jaymar was derived from the name JAcob MARx and then known as Jaymar Specialty Company. Louis Marx Company is no longer in business, but in 1993 Jaymar was still manufacturing toy pianos, benches, and other wood products in the USA, and importing musical and other toys. They no longer import toy sewing machines. Information furnished by Frank Trinca, President.

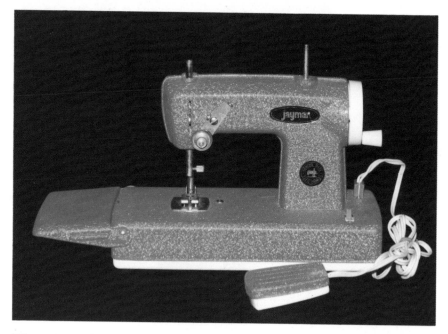

Plate 207. This JAYMAR is all metal and finished in orange crinkle paint. Features are: battery operated, foot pedal, on/off switch, tension regulator, and extension table. The trademark of a diamond shape with "C. K." written inside appears on the bottom. Made in Japan. 6½"h x 4"d x 8"w.

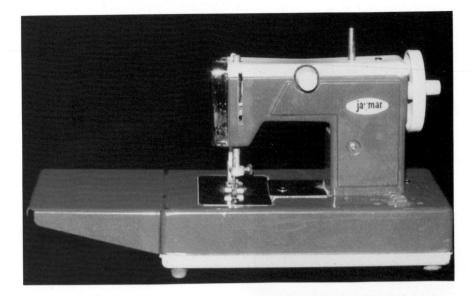

Plate 208. This bright red and white metal JAYMAR is battery operated with an on/off switch. Extension table is attached. Made in Japan. 5½"h x 4"d x 7"w.

Plate 209. This JAYMAR is all metal except for a white plastic base, and white plastic presser foot. The face plate is shaped differently from the previous photograph and the sewing plate is smaller. It is battery operated with an on/off switch, and has an extension table. Made in Japan. 5½"h x 4"w x 7"d.

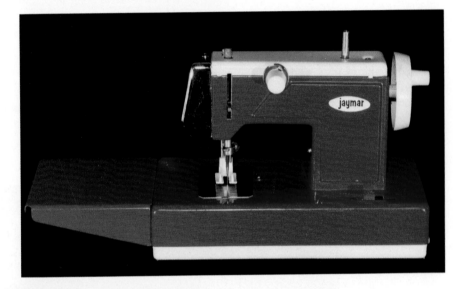

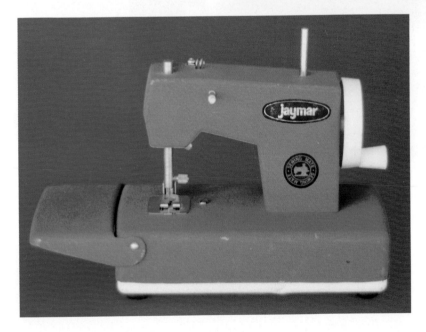

Plate 210. This JAYMAR is manually operated. The diamond trademark with CK inside is stamped underneath. The metal machine is finished with dark blue crinkle paint. Extension table is attached. Made in Japan. Toy from collection of Wanda Wilson. 5½"h x 4"d x 7¾"w.

KAYanEE CORPORATION of AMERICA
New York, New York USA

"BERLIN, Made in Germany –U. S. Zone" is stamped on this brand. After World War II, Germany was divided into zones: American, British, French, and Soviet,. The zones remained for approximately four years, however, the KAYanEE toy sewing machines were still stamped US Zone many years later. Some of the boxes have an address with US Postal Zones (example—New York 10, N. Y.). These postal zones began in 1943, and were replaced by zip codes in 1963. Boxes have been found with the zip code indicating they were distributed after 1963. Many KAYanEEs were offered in the Montgomery Ward Christmas Catalogs of 1954 through 1963. Also, several models appeared in the 1965 and 1966 J. C. Penney Christmas Catalogs.

If you examine these toys, some may have an "M" stamped underneath, indicating F.W. Müller Company, that marketed this brand. Their factory was located in the US Zone of Germany, and closed in 1979.

KAYanEE or Sew Master were marked on these toys. The trademark is a circle similar to a world globe with "KAYanEE, Reg. U.S. Trademark" written inside. Many colors and styles were available. Even the name was written in different styles, with printing or script. Some have single sheet metal bodies with an exposed mechanism. They came with raised sewing plates, free arms, tiny drawers, and extension tables. Some used batteries or electricity, but the majority were manually operated. Beautiful flowers appeared on many of the bodies and bases. Others were plain with one, two, or three ridges on the body. Several may appear indentical in the photographs, but note the difference in size. All machines were made post World War II.

Plate 211. KAYanEE SEW MASTER, hand operated, single sheet metal body. 6"h x 4⅜"d x 7⅛"w.

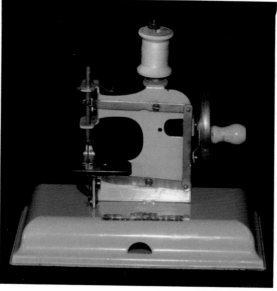

Plate 212. KAYanEE SEW MASTER, hand operated, single sheet metal body. 6"h x 4⅜"d x 7⅛"w.

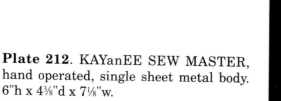

Plate 213. KAYanEE SEW MASTER, hand operated, single sheet metal body, shown with box and clamp. Toy from collection of Glenda Scott. 6"h x 4⅜"d x 7⅛"w.

Plate 214. KAYanEE SEW MASTER, hand operated, single sheet metal body, decorated with flowers. Toy from collection of Glenda Scott. 6"h x 4⅜"d x 7⅛"w.

Plate 215. KAYanEE SEW MASTER, hand operated, single sheet metal body, decorated with flowers. 6"h x 4⅜"d x 7⅛"w.

Plate 216. KAYanEE SEW MASTER, hand operated, single sheet metal body, decorated with flowers. 6"h x 4⅜"d x 7⅛"w.

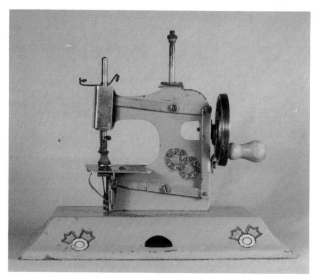

Plate 217. KAYanEE SEW MASTER, hand operated, single sheet metal body, decorated with medallions and tiny floral wreaths. Photograph courtesy of Joe and Evelyn Watkins. 6"h x 4⅜"d x 7⅛"w.

Plate 218. KAYanEE SEW MASTER, hand operated, double sheet metal body, spool pin slanted. 5"h x 4⅜"d x 7⅛"w.

Plate 219. KAYanEE SEW MASTER, hand operated, double sheet metal body, enlarged sewing plate. 6½"h x 4⅜"d x 7¾"w.

Plate 220. KAYanEE SEW MASTER, hand operated, double sheet metal body. 6"h x 4⅜"d x 7⅛"w.

Plate 221. SEWMASTER (written in script) on top of base, hand operated, floral design. Toy from collection of Wanda Wilson. 6¾"h x 4⅝"d x 8"w.

Plate 222. No label shown, hand operated, floral design. 7"h x 4⅜"d x 8½"w.

Plate 223. SEWMASTER (written in script), hand operated, floral design. Toy from collection of Glenda Scott. 7"h x 4½"d x 8¾"w.

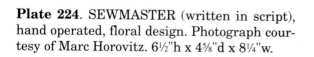

Plate 224. SEWMASTER (written in script), hand operated, floral design. Photograph courtesy of Marc Horovitz. 6½"h x 4⅝"d x 8¼"w.

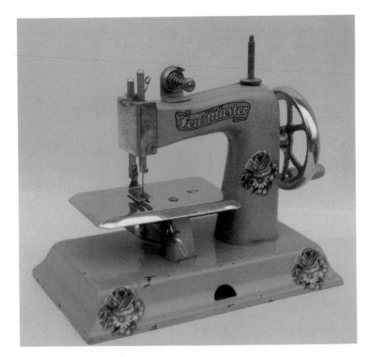

Plate 225. SEW MASTER (written in script), hand operated, floral design. Photograph courtesy of Marc Horovitz. 6½"h x 4⅝"d x 8¼"w.

Plate 226. SEW MASTER (in script on base), hand operated, floral designs. Photograph courtesy of Marc Horovitz. 6½"h x 4⅝"d x 8¼"w.

Plate 227. SEWMASTER (written in script), hand operated, floral design. Toy from collection of Glenda Scott. 7"h x 4½"d x 8¾"w.

Plate 228. KAYanEE SEW MASTER, hand operated, shown with original box. 5¾"h x 4⅜"d x 7¾"w.

Plate 229. KAYanEE SEW MASTER, hand operated. 6"h x 4⅜"d x 8¼"w.

Plate 230. SEW MASTER (written in script), hand operated, handwheel has spokes. 6½"h x 4⅜"d x 8¼"w.

Plate 231. SEW MASTER, hand operated, two-tone color. 6¾"h x 4⅜"d x 7¾"w.

Plate 232. KAYanEE SEW MASTER, hand operated, two-tone color. 6¾"h x 4⅜"d x 7¾"w.

Plate 233. SEW MASTER, hand operated, trademark shown on body. 6"h x 4⅜"d x 8¼"w.

Plate 234. SEW MASTER, battery operated, on/off switch, trademark shown on body. 6"h x 4⅜"d x 8¼"w.

Plate 235. KAYanEE SEW MASTER, hand operated. 6¼"h x 4¾"d x 8¼"w.

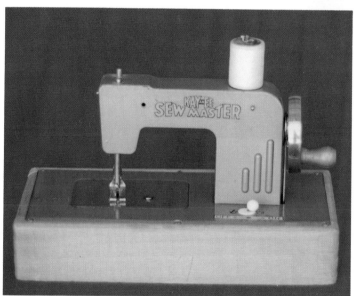

Plate 236. KAYanEE SEW MASTER, battery operated, on/off switch, wood base, three ridges on body. 6"h x 4½"d x 8½"w.

Plate 237. KAYanEE SEW MASTER, battery operated, on/off switch, wood base, three ridges on body. 6"h x 4¼"d x 7¾"w.

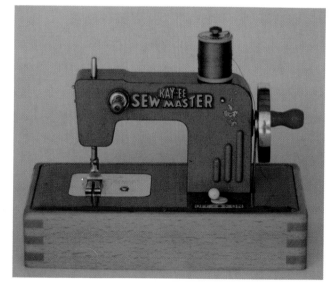

Plate 238. KAYanEE SEW MASTER, battery operated, on/off switch, wood base, three ridges on body. 6"h x 4¼"d x 7¾"w.

Plate 239. KAYanEE SEW MASTER, hand operated, wood base, three ridges on body. 6"h x 4¼"d x 7¾"w.

Plate 240. KAYanEE SEW MASTER, hand operated, wood base, three ridges on body. 6"h x 4¼"d x 7¾"w.

Plate 241. KAYanEE SEW MASTER, battery operated, on/off switch, wood base, three ridges on body. 6¼"h x 4½"d x 8½"w.

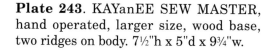

Plate 242. KAYanEE SEW MASTER, battery operated, on/off switch, wood base, three ridges on body. 6"h x 4¼"d x 7¾"w.

Plate 243. KAYanEE SEW MASTER, hand operated, larger size, wood base, two ridges on body. 7½"h x 5"d x 9¾"w.

Plate 244. KAYanEE SEW MASTER, hand operated, wood base, two ridges on body. 6½"h x 4½"d x 8½"w.

Plate 245.KAYanEE SEW MASTER, hand operated, wood base with two ridges. 6½"h x 4⅜"d x 8½"w.

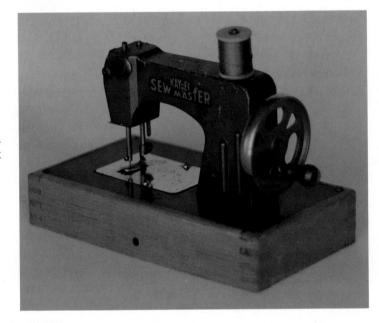

Plate 246. SEW MASTER (written in script), hand operated, larger size, wood base, two ridges on body. 7½"h x 5"d x 9¾"w.

Plate 247. KAYanEE SEW MASTER, battery operated, on/off switch, wood base. 6"h x 4½"d x 8½"w.

Plate 248. KAYanEE SEW MASTER, battery operated, on/off switch, wood base. 6"h x 4¼"d x 7¾"w.

Plate 249. SEW MASTER, battery operated, on/off switch and foot pedal, wood base with drawer, body has trademark emblem. 7"h x 5¼"d x 9½"w.

Plate 250. SEW MASTER, battery operated, on/off switch, trademark emblem on body, wood base with extension table (4¼" x 3½"). Photograph courtesy of Peggy Foust. 6"h x 5"d x 9¾"w.

Plate 251. KAYanEE SEW MASTER, battery operated, on/off switch, wood base, free arm style, spool pin on front. 7"h x 4½"d x 8½"w.

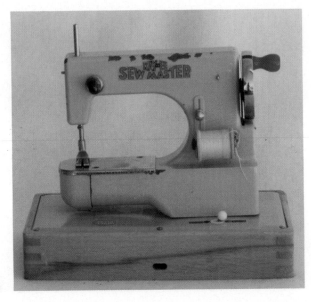

Plate 252. KAYanEE SEW MASTER, battery operated, on/off switch, wood base, free arm style, spool pin on front. Toy from collection of Glenda Scott. 8"h x 4¾"d x 8¾"w.

Plate 253 and 253A. KAYanEE SEW MASTER, front and back view. Electric, motor on back, on/off switch, wood base with tiny drawer. 7"h x 5"d x 9¾"w.

Kochs–Adler Company
Bielefeld, Germany

In 1860 Carl Baer and Heinrich Koch began a sewing machine company under the name Baer and Koch. The firm changed names over the years as partners resigned or died, and others were added. The company made much progress and the name Koch on sewing machines gradually became known the world over. In 1890 they adopted the use of a rotary shuttle which was incorporated into a range of machines under the name Adler (eagle) which brought them world recognition. The factory sustained much damage during World War II, but after the war, trade was soon back to normal. The Kochs-Adler Company was most noted for sewing machines for boots and heavy leather goods, but after 1950, they produced other sewing machines for the clothing industry. Reference: *An International History of the Sewing Machine* by Frank P. Godfrey. ISBN 0 7091 98760. Robert Hale Ltd., London.

Plate 254. This ADLER is stamped "Made in Western Germany." The metal machine is mounted on a wood base that requires a clamp. It is unknown to this author if this toy was manufactured by Kochs-Adler or by another firm for them. Photograph courtesy of Judy Arnold. 8⅛"h x 4⅜"d x 8¼"w; c. post WWII.

Benoit Lakner
Paris, France

Plate 255. LE FAVOURITE is a toy made in France by Benoit Lakner, Paris, Bvd. Voltaire 198 Patent 105269-13, October 1874. It is made of cast iron with a dragon cast in the frame and has gold decorations and a painted picture of a minstrel. Information reference: *Old French Sewing Machines* by Peter Wilhelm. Photograph courtesy of Maggie Snell. c. 1874.

LANARD TOYS, Ltd.
200 5th Ave.
New York, NY USA

Plate 256 and 256A. The plastic SIMPLICITY SEWING MACHINE, Model 8078, works without a needle. Yarn and medium weight paper are used. It is battery operated with a foot pedal and is recommended for ages 4 and over. The toy came trimmed in several shades of pink or aqua, and had a small drawer for accessories. Information on the box is: "1986 Lanard Toys, Ltd–Made in Macau–Distributed by Super Distributors, Jefferson, LA. 70001. Simplicity is a registered trademark of Simplicity Pattern Co., Inc., New York, NY. " The J. C. Penney Christmas Catalog of 1989, featured this toy that sold for $12.99. 7½"h x 4½"d x 8¼"w; c. 1980s.

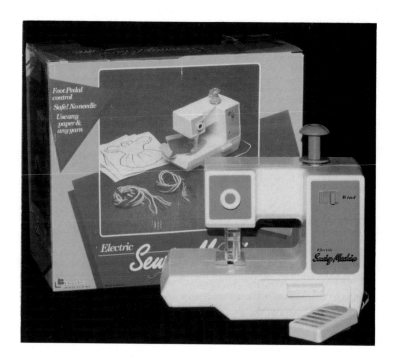

Plate 257. This plastic LANARD toy, model No. 8079, just says "Electric Sewing Machine." Simplicity is not listed on it. The toy is safe with no exposed sharp points and uses yarn and paper. Many paper patterns were included. It is battery operated with a foot pedal and has a small drawer for accessories. Made in Macau. Recommended for ages 4 and up. 7½"h x 4½"d x 8¼"w; c. 1990s.

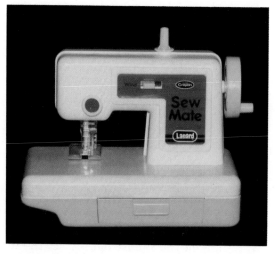

Plate 258. SEW MATE is a plastic Lanard toy. No battery is necessary. It is hand operated without a needle and uses yarn and paper. A small drawer is provided for storing accessories. The trademark "A Mel Appel CRAYON" is on the machine. Made in Hong Kong. The spool for yarn is missing in the photograph. 7½"h x 4½"d x 8¼"w; c. 1980s.

Liliputian

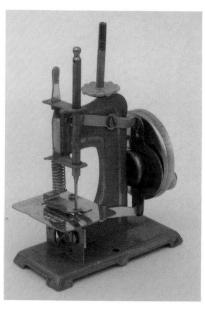

Plate 259 and Plate 259A. The tiny metal LILIPUTIAN was available in various colors: black, blue, dark turquoise, and rust. "D. R. G. M." and "The Liliputian, Smallest Sewing Machine in the World—Watch it Sew" is written on the front of the box. Instructions say to fasten machine to table or board with two screws. "Made in Germany—Vielfach Geschutz" is printed on the the sewing plate. Photograph of blue machine courtesy of Marc Horovitz. Photograph of black machine courtesy of Joseph and Louisa Llull. 3"h x 1⅜"d x 2½"w; c. pre WWII.

LINDSTROM TOOL & TOY CO.
50 Silliman Ave.
Bridgeport, Connecticut USA
Frank L. Lindstrom, President

This is a quote from an article from *The Bridgeport Sunday Post*, December 15, 1940:

LOCAL PLANTS RUSHED AS WAR CURTAILS IMPORTS AND PLAYTHINGS

"And you ought to see the toy-model sewing machines the local factory is making for Santa by the truck-load. Small-scale, artfully lithographed, this machine is hand operated from a flywheel crank and is equipped with needle, thread, a clamp for securing the machine to a table—a streamlined item on the Lindstrom list." Newspaper article furnished by Robert Brucato.

This company is no longer in business.

Many of the Lindstrom toy sewing machines were labeled "Little Miss." The famous child movie star, Shirley Temple, starred in the smash hits, "Little Miss Marker" in 1943, and "Little Miss Broadway" in 1938. These toy sewing machines were named after this famous star. One model shows the beautiful child's face with blond curls. Movie reference: *Child Star, An Autobiography* by Shirley Temple Black.

Plate 260. This sheet metal lithographed toy has no name or patent on the machine, but a box says: "Lindstrom's LITTLE MISS Sewing Machine #203—Hand operated—Manf. by the Lindstrom Tool & Toy Co. Bridgeport, Conn.—Made in USA—Pat. 1,809,192." The patent was issued to R. E. Cahill and John Caferini, inventors, on July 9, 1931. The picture on the patent bears no resemblance to this toy sewing machine. 7¼"h x 5"d x 8¼"w; c. 1930s and 1940s.

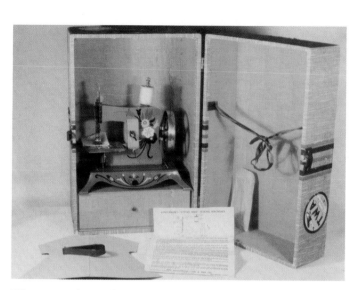

Plate 260A. and 260B. The Lindstrom LITTLE MISS #203 was available in a traveling case. Photograph courtesy of Joe and Evelyn Watkins.

Plate 261. "LINDSTROM, MADE IN USA, PATENTED 1,809,192, and 2,048,555" is printed on the front of this lithographed toy. The second patent number is dated July 21, 1936, and issued to Frank L. Lindstrom. The first paragraph of the patent says: "This invention relates to new and useful improvements in sewing machines and has particular relation to small sewing machines of the type that may be regarded as toys although capable of performing actual sewing operations. An object of this invention is to provide a sewing machine of the class indicated and which may be manufactured at low costs." This toy is highly decorated with flowers, made of metal, and hand operated. 7¼"h x 5"d x 8¼"w; c. 1930s and 1940s.

Plate 262. "LINDSTROM, Made in USA, Patented 1,809,192" is printed on the front. This elegant hand operated metal toy has golden flowers and a blonde girl with "Little Miss" printed under her picture. This "Little Miss" is Shirley Temple. The Sears Christmas Catalogs of 1936 and 1937, featured this toy. 7¼"h x 5"d x 8¼"w; c. 1930s.

Plate 263. This LINDSTROM "LITTLE MISS" is identical to the previous photograph except it has two patent numbers listed – 1,809,192 and 2,048, 555. Toy from collection of Wanda Wilson. 7¼"h x 5"d x 8¼"w; c. 1930s and 1940s.

Plate 264. The electric LITTLE MISS, has a red decal on the base that says: "Lindstrom's Little Miss Electric Sewing Machine, Model No. 210, mfg. by Lindstrom Tool and Toy Co. Bridgeport, Conn.— for use with 115 volt 60 cycle alternating current." The "Little Miss" depicted is Shirley Temple. Sears Christmas Catalogs of 1936 and 1937, featured this electric toy. 7¼"h x 7"d x 8¼"w; c. 1930s.

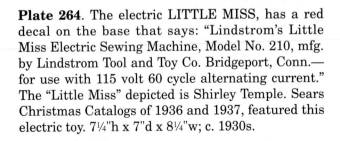

Plate 265. The woodgrain LINDSTROM is very elegant. It is all metal and hand operated. Photograph courtesy of Joe and Evelyn Watkins. 7¼"h 5"d x 8¼"w; c. 1930s and 1940s.

Plate 266. The woodgrain LINDSTROM was also available with an electric motor. Photograph courtesy of James and Sandra Seymour. 8"h x 6½"d x 8¼"w; c. 1930s and 1940s.

Little Mary Mix Up

Plate 267. The LITTLE MARY MIX UP sewing machine is from Joseph Schneider, Inc. It is unknown to this author if this was the manufacturer or the distributor. The machine has no identifying marks. It has a single sheet metal body, solid geared handwheel without spokes, and table clamp. The 1934 and 1935 Sears, Roebuck, and Co., Catalogs showed a green toy sewing machine with the same markings and size for $1.00. Toy from collection of Wanda Wilson. 7"h x 3¾"d x 7¾"w; c. 1930s.

Plate 268. This green toy has a slightly different body design than the previous photograph, but the mechanism appears the same. The handwheel has spokes. 7"h x 3¾"d x 7¾"w; c. 1930s.

Plate 269. This green toy is the same as the bottom photograph on the previous page, except the handwheel has spokes. 7"h x 3¾"d x 7¾"w; c. 1930s.

L. J. N. Toys, Ltd.
New York, N.Y. USA

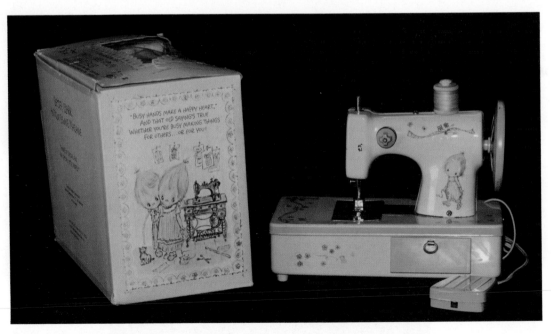

Plate 270. BETSEY CLARK, Model No. 8100, was distributed by L.J.N. Toys, Ltd. This toy was made in Hong Kong and bears the trademark of Hallmark Cards, Inc., 1973, 1975, 1976. The J.C. Penney Christmas Catalog of 1976, featured this all metal sewing machine, however the name was spelled Betsy in the catalog, and the box says Betsey. Original selling price was $9.99. Special features are: battery operation, storage drawer, foot pedal, light, sews a straight chain stitch, and was recommended for ages 8 and up. A charming poem on the box reads: "Busy hands make a happy heart, and that old saying is true whether you're busy making things for others …or for you!" The 1976 Montgomery Ward Christmas Catalog featured an all plastic toy that looks identical to this one for $9.99. 6½" h x 4¼"d x 7¾"w; c. 1970s.

Plate 271. This toy is totally unmarked except for a small sticker underneath that says "Made in Hong Kong." The style of the machine is identical to the Betsey Clark model made by L.J.N. Toys, but that company is not marked on this toy. A box does not have manufacturing information. The lovely girl in the yellow dress with the yellow bow in her hair is very similar to the Precious Moments series by Enesco. The toy is made of plastic and metal and is battery operated with a foot pedal. 6¼"h x 4"d x 7¾"w.

Louis Marx Company

Louis Marx was born 1896, in Brooklyn, New York. He began working for toy companies in his teens, then later started his own firm. In approximately 1920, mass production of toys began. By 1940, he had became the largest toy manufacturer in the world. At age 76, he sold his entire outlay to Quaker Oats Co. After a few years, the firm sold to a British company, Dunbee-Combex. This firm filed bankruptcy in 1980. Reference: Greenberg's Guide to Marx Toys, volume 1 by Maxine A. Pinsky. ISBN#0-8977-027-2.

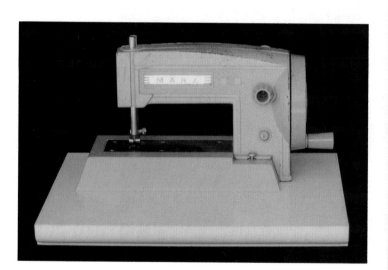

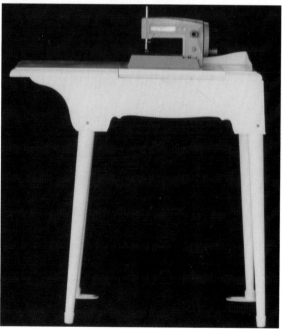

Plate 272 and 272A. MARX SEW BIG is a die-cast, blue finished metal, hand operated toy for the junior seamstress. It has a two foot high convertible ivory plastic table. The 10" square machine platform flips down to make a desk. A round blue plastic storage hassock, 13" high, accompanied the toy. J. C. Penney and Montgomery Ward Christmas Catalogs of 1966, offered this Marx toy and accessories. Machine only: 5"h x 4¾"d x 8½"w; c. 1960s.

Mattel, Inc.
El Segundo, California

In approximately 1945, Harold Matson and Elliot Handler started Mattel. "Matt" for Matson and "el" for Elliot formed the name Mattel. They incorporated in 1948, in California. Ruth Handler, Elliot's wife initiated the Barbie Doll that was named after their daughter. This is now the most famous doll in the world. Several toy sewing machines have been designed for the Barbie doll house and other machines came with Barbie doll and patterns. Reference: *Modern Toys American Toys 1930-1980* by Linda Baker, A Collector Book.

Plate 273. SEW MAGIC is featured in the J. C. Penney Christmas Catalogs of 1973, 1974, and 1975. The ad says: "No needle—just a little magic makes pattern pieces stick together. Just pop in the special cartridge, and you are ready—liquid formula in cartridge joins fabric fast." Fabric, decorations for four Barbie doll outfits, dress form, and sewing hints by McCall patterns were included. Any Barbie memorabilia is very desirable to collectors, making this toy more valuable. The plastic machine requires batteries. Information on box: "#7723, Made in Mexico, 1973 Mattel, Inc., Hawthorn, California. Not recommended for children under 4." 5¼"h x 5"d x 9"w; c. 1970s.

Plate 274. SEW MAGIC deluxe set by Mattel is identical to the previous photograph, however it does not say Barbie. c. 1970s.

Plate 275. SEW by Mattel was manufactured in Mexico. This plastic toy was made for a toddler. Pull the string behind the red button, and it makes a rhythmic sound of sewing as the fake needle goes up and down. "TUFF STUFF" is written on the back side. 6½"h x 3¾"d x 7¼"w; c. 1970s.

Plate 276. SEW PERFECT is battery operated with an on/off switch and is made of plastic and metal. J. C. Penney Christmas Catalogs from 1977 through 1982, and the Montgomery Ward Christmas Catalogs from 1977 through 1980, offered this toy. Penney's advertisement says, "Snap in the cassette and you are ready to chain-stitch. Needle and thread are fully enclosed in see-through plastic. Bobbin attachment lets you hem and add trim in one step. Includes cassette with 300' of thread, bobbin with 10' of trim, 6 Simplicity projects, enough fabric for a stuffed animal." Information on box: "#9849, Mattel, Inc." Hawthorn, California, Made in USA, Recommended for ages over 6." 7"h x 5¾"d x 9¾"w; c. 1970s and 1980s.

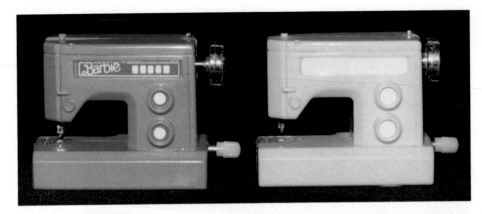

Plate 277. Barbie enthusiasts will love these tiny sewing machines that are recommended for ages 3 and over. Just wind it up, and the needle moves up and down, but does not actually sew. The package offers the following information: "#7936, Arco Toys, LTD., a Mattel Company, Westbury, New York, Made in China. Barbie is a trademark owned by and used under license from Mattel, Inc." 1½"h x 1⅛"d x 2¼"w; c.1980s and 1990s.

Metallograph Corp.
(Also see Sotoy)

Plate 278. "BABY GRAND Sewing Machine—Manufactured by The Metallograph Corp., New York, NY—patent applied for" is printed on the front of this metal machine. It will operate by handwheel, however a groove is in the handwheel indicating it may be operated by a belt. Photograph courtesy of Joe and Evelyn Watkins. 6⅛"h x 3¾"d x 6¾"w; c. early 1900s.

Montgomery Ward, Inc.
Signature, a trade name used by Montgomery Ward

Plate 279. This SIGNATURE JUNIOR was first featured in the Montgomery Ward Christmas Catalog in 1965. "Made in Japan" is stamped on the bottom. Features are: die-cast head, plastic base and carrying case, electric A/C 110 volt, foot pedal, and sewing light. 7½"h x 5½"d x 11¼"w; c. 1960s.

Plate 280 and 280A. This SIGNATURE JUNIOR is all metal with a crackle finish. It was available in several two-tone colors. Features are: manual or battery operated, on/off switch, foot pedal, tension and stitch length regulator, and extension table (not shown). 6½"h x 4"d x 8"w; c. 1960s.

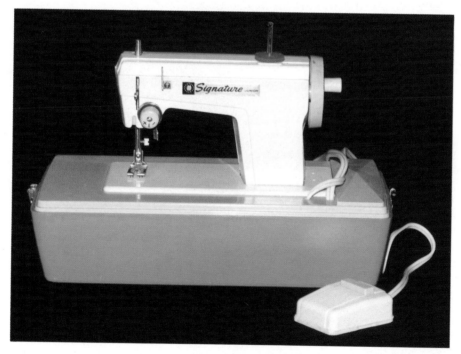

Plate 281. This SIGNATURE JUNIOR was featured in many issues of the Montgomery Ward Christmas Catalogs during the 1960s. "Article No. 48-32275, Model No. AST-32275-A," and "Made in Japan" are written on the bottom. The toy is electric A/C 110 volt and has a plastic snap-on cover. 8"h x 5¼"d x 11¼"w; c. 1960s.

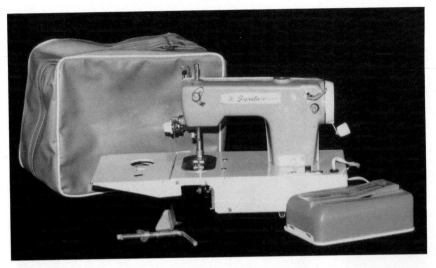

Plate 282. "A Ward's Exclusive" is the advertisement for this SIGNATURE JUNIOR. It is a lockstitch machine that operates like a regular machine. "Original Sew-ette Japan" is stamped on the sewing plate. It is battery operated with an extra large foot pedal that holds the batteries. Other features are: soft vinyl zippered case, switch for filling the bobbin or sewing, extension table (3½" x 5¼"), table clamp, round bobbin, tension regulator, and fold out handle on the wheel for manual operation. 7"h x 5½"d x 8"w; c.1960s.

Plate 283. "B/O SEWING MACHINE, Regular Stitch" is written on the box of this SIGNATURE JUNIOR. "Original Sew-ette Japan" is stamped on the sewing plate. Features are: battery operated with on/off switch and foot pedal, sews a lockstitch, has round bobbin, tension regulator, and extension table (3½" x 5¼"). It has another switch for filling the bobbin or sewing. A small handle on the wheel folds out for manual use. 7½"h x 5¼"d x 8"w; c. 1960s.

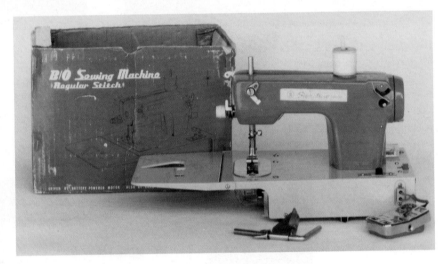

Plate 284. This blue metal hand operated SIGNATURE JUNIOR was offered in the 1967 Montgomery Ward Christmas Catalog with an apron kit for $4.99. Note the box has the Casige Eagle trademark on it indicating that this toy was made in Germany. Photograph courtesy of Judy Arnold. 6"h x 4⅞"d x 8⅜"w; c. 1960s.

Plate 285. "Ward's own Signature sewing machine permanently mounted on child-size table" is the way the Montgomery Ward Christmas Catalog of 1968, advertised this toy that sold for $19.99. Table, smoothly finished in oak veneer, has a drawer for accessories. The machine has an enameled steel head, is manual or battery operated with a foot pedal, and sews a chain stitch. "Made in Western Germany" is stamped on the sewing plate. Photograph courtesy of Peggy Foust. Table: 23"h x 10½"d x 22½"w; machine: 8"w; c. 1968.

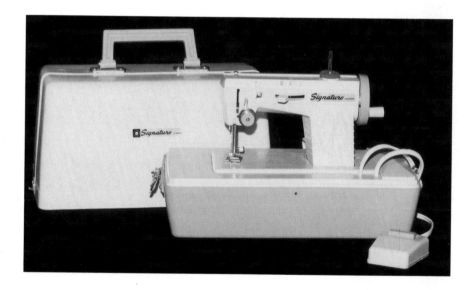

Plate 286. This zig-zag SIGNATURE JUNIOR was first offered in the Montgomery Ward Christmas Catalog in 1970. "Saitama Model No. MZ-1 and Made in Japan" are marked on the bottom. Features are: die-cast metal and plastic head, plastic base and cover, tension regulator, switch for zig-zag or straight stitch, electric A/C 110 volt, and foot pedal. 8"h x 5½"d x 11¼"w; c. 1970s.

Plate 287. "Distributed by Montgomery Ward & Co., Inc., Chicago, IL. 60607" is written on the bottom of this two-tone blue plastic toy. "Made in Japan" is also stamped on the bottom. This toy was offered in the Montgomery Ward Christmas Catalogs for several years in the 1970s. It was advertised for beginners and not recommended for ages under 5. The mechanism is manually or battery operated with a foot pedal. 6¾"h x 4¼"d x 8¾"w; c. 1970s.

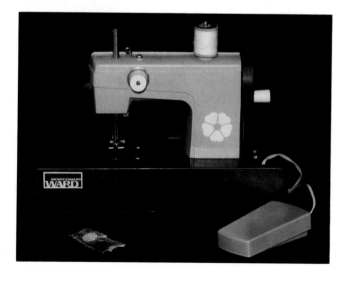

Plate 288 and 288A. The metal emblems on these machines have M. W. on them. "Made in Japan" is printed on the body. This machine can be operated in two ways: by the belt drive wheel or the battery powered electric motor which is gear driven with a clutch assembly that engages to turn the complete mechanism. It has an on/off switch, and one toy has a switch for a light. This toy is almost identical to the Morse machine made in Japan. 7"h x 5¼"d x 11¼"w.

Morse Sewing Machine & Supply Corp.

The September 1954 issue of *Good Housekeeping* Magazine contained an advertisement for Morse adult domestic machines. Two addresses were listed: 40-42 West 27th Street, New York, New York, and 2615 West Pico Blvd., Los Angeles, California. The ad says: "The revolutionary Morse machines are made in the precision plant at Nagoya, Japan."

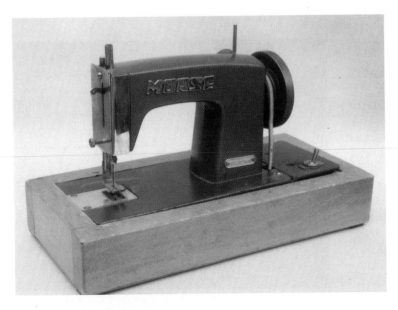

Plate 289. The mechanism of this MORSE machine can be utilized in two ways. It may be operated by the belt drive wheel. When turned clockwise, this does not engage the electric motor. The battery powered electric motor is gear driven with a clutch assembly that engages to turn the complete mechanism. It has an on/off switch. This is a very well engineered toy. The body is cast metal and mounted on a wood base. A small attached plate on the front says "Made in Japan." Photograph courtesy of Marc Horovitz. 6¼"h x 5¼"d x 11½"w.

Plate 324A. These LITTLE WORKER machines show slightly different decorations. Photograph courtesy of Conrad and Jo Ann Overton.

Plate 325. This small NEW HOME (Midget) is almost identical to the Little Worker. It was also marketed as a practical sewing machine or portable for travelers. Photograph courtesy of Frank Smith, Antique Sewing Machine Museum. 10½"h x 6"d x 10½"w; c. early 1900s.

Plate 326. This small NEW HOME was probably a promotional item. The plastic machine is very heavy for its size. It does not sew and could be used for a paper weight. 2"h x 1¼"d x 2¾"w.

J. C. Penney Company, Inc.

Plate 327. Penney's portable electric sewing machines were modeled after Penney's own Penncrest Sewing Machines for mother. Plastic carrying case snaps into place. Features include: die-cast metal head, plastic base, metal and nylon gears, foot operated on/off pedal, light, and thread-tension adjustment knob. It sews a single thread chain stitch. Imported from Japan. J. C. Penney Christmas Catalogs from 1967 to 1970, featured this toy for $16.44 and $16.88. 7¾"h x 5½"d x 11"w; c. 1960s and 1970s.

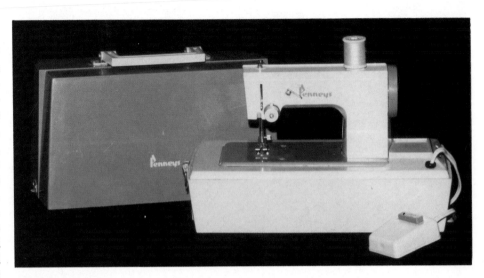

Plate 328.Penney's hand operated toy delighted the young sewer who was not ready for the speed of an electric model. It has a high quality metal head and metal gears. The bright red toy came equipped with needle guide, thread tension adjustment, and clamp to fasten to table. J. C. Penney Christmas Catalogs of 1976 thru 1970, featured this toy for $3.88. 6¼"h x 3¾"d x 7¾"w; c. 1960s and 1970s.

Plate 329. Distributed by J. C. Penney Co. and manufactured in Japan, this toy can be used three ways: with AC adapter, by battery, or hand operated, and has a sewing light and foot pedal. It sews a single thread chain stitch, has die-cast metal head and plastic base with metal and nylon gears. This toy was featured in the J. C. Penney Christmas Catalog of 1971, for $13.77, and in 1973 for $14.98. Toy from collection of Janice Starkey. 7⅛"h x 5⅜"d x 10⅝"w; c. 1970s.

Pfaff

Parent company location: Kaiserslautern, Germany

George Michael Pfaff, founder, was born 1823 and died 1893. In his early years, he worked with his father and brothers building musical instruments in Germany. During his visit to the World's Fair in London in 1850, he had the opportunity to study a new machine that sewed. The fascination for the sewing machine never left him. In 1862, he built his first sewing machine. His company, which grew up from very modest beginnings, is today one of the largest sewing machine manufacturers in Europe, and is represented in more than 130 countries of the world. 1987 was the 125th anniversary of Pfaff. Today, industrial machines represent two-thirds and domestic machines one-third of the total business.
Information furnished by: Pfaff American Sales Corp., Paramus, New Jersey.

Plate 330. The PFAFF free arm toy has a modern design. A small battery is required for the light, but the machine is hand operated. This is an exceptionally well made machine. In 1956, J.C. Penney Christmas catalog offered a sewing kit that included a small plastic Pfaff toy sewing machine with a free arm designed just like this metal toy. Other toy models were available but it is not known to this author if Pfaff actually manufactured these or if another firm made these for Pfaff. Photograph courtesy of Marc Horovitz. 6"h x 4"d x 7"w.

Ernst Plank

Ernst Plank distributed toys in Germany. *The Official Identification and Price Guide to Collectible Toys* written by Richard Fritz, 5th edition gives the following information: founder: Ernst Plank, Nuremberg, Germany, 1866-1930; specialty: tin trains, airplanes, boats, automobiles.

Plate 331. "VICTORIA" is printed on the box of this toy distributed by Ernst Plank. Many other ornate Victorian style machines were available. They also came in colors including red and blue. An oval shaped trademark with EP is engraved on the metal machines. Photograph courtesy of Judy Arnold. 6½"h x 4¼"d x 6¼"w; c. pre WWII.

Pony

Plate 332 and 332A. The PONY is desired by collectors and is considered relatively scarce. The Montgomery Ward Catalog of 1904, offered this toy for $1.50. The ad says: "Especially adapted for kindergarten use." It is elegantly enameled and finished in floral designs of different colors. Wilcox and Gibbs self-setting needles are used. A table clamp accompanied the toy. This author has no proof of manufacturer, however, note the cone shaped tension. It is very similar to the Foley and Williams machines. Also the floral designs are the same as on the Foley and Williams Midget. Photograph courtesy of Marjorie Abel. 8"h x 2½"d x 7½"w; c. early 1900s.

Schürhoff and Co.

Schürhoff and Co. made bicycles and began the manufacture of toy sewing machines in Gevelsberg, Germany, after WWII from 1948 to 1957. Approximately nine models were produced, and today these are eagerly sought by collectors. Information furnished by Georg Reinfelder.

Plate 333. and 333A. Gold Rain from an old German fairy story is the theme for this SCHÜRHOFF ORIGINAL DIANA. The splendid details are on the front and back side. The green toy also has designs on each corner of the base and has a red handwheel. Photograph of front side and information courtesy Georg Reinfelder. Photo of back side from collection of Glenda Scott. 6½"h x 4½"d x 8½"w; c. 1950s.

Sears, Roebuck, & Company
Sears
Kenmore (A tradename used on Sears Products.)

Plate 334. National Sewing Machine Company manufactured this KENMORE. The toy is made of metal, painted bright red, and mounted on a wood base that is secured with a table clamp. The head tilts backward to reveal a chain driven mechanism. Photograph courtesy of Robert Brucato. 6½"h x 4⅛"d x 9"w; c. 1930s and 1940s.

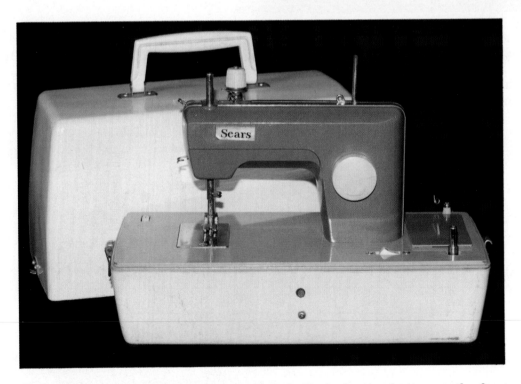

Plate 335. This SEARS toy sews a lockstitch. Push the tiny button on the front, and the head tilts backward to reveal the mechanism and to insert the bobbin. Other features are: plastic cover, small storage compartment, battery operated, on/off switch, and tension regulator. The toy has a metal head and plastic base. 8"h x 5½"d x 11¼"w.

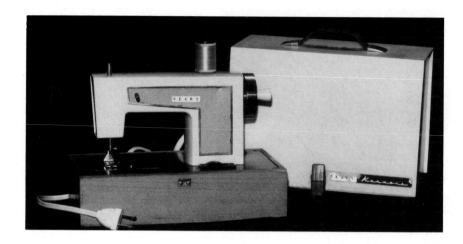

Plate 336. This SEARS toy is electric (A/C 110 volt). The plastic cover also has the KENMORE name. "Made in Berlin, Germany, U.S. zone" is stamped on the sewing plate. The metal machine is mounted on a wood base and operated with an on/off switch. 7"h x 5"d x 8½"w; c. post WWII.

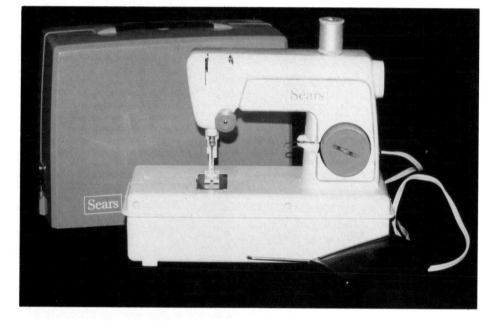

Plate 337. and 337A. This SEARS toy, model No. 49-1210, has a bobbin and sews a lockstitch. Other features are: battery operated, foot pedal, pink plastic carrying cover, attached table clamp, and hand crank that snaps in for manual operation. Made in France. 9"h x 4½"d x 10"w; c. 1960s and 1970s.

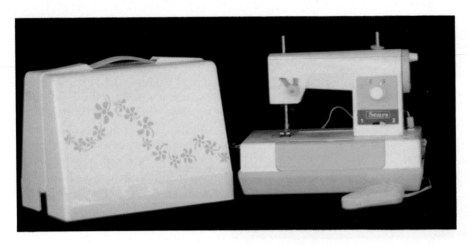

Plate 338. This SEARS toy sews a zig-zag or straight stitch. Features are: metal head, plastic base, plastic snap on carrying case, battery operated, foot pedal, on/off switch, stitch length and tension regulator. It was made in Japan by Crystal Sewing Machine Industrial Co., Ltd. Toy from collection of Janice Starkey. 8½"hx 6½"d x 10"w.

Sew-Ette

Plate 339. "SEW-ETTE" is written in red plastic script letters. The toy is metal with blue crinkle finish. Features are: battery operated, on/off switch, foot pedal (not shown), extension table (not shown), tension and stitch length regulator. Made in Japan. Toy from collection of Wanda Wilson. 5½"h x 4"d x 7⅞"w; c. 1960s.

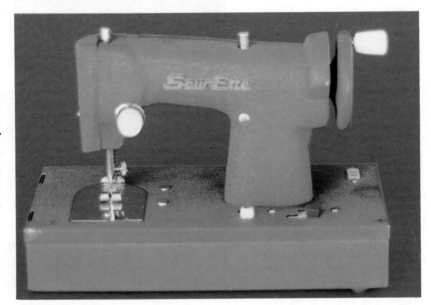

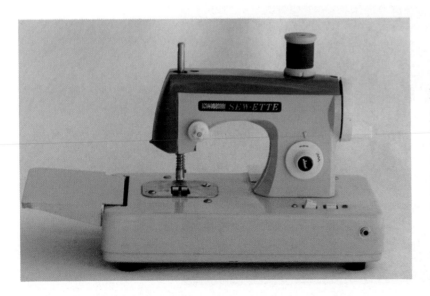

Plate 340. This SEW-ETTE is a zig-zag machine. "Ideal" is written on the knob that changes from zig-zag to straight stitches. The toy is battery operated with on/off switch. Made in Japan. Toy from collection of Glenda Scott. 7"h x 5¼"d x 11¼"w (includes extension table).

Plate 341. "SEW-ETTE" is written in metal script letters on this two-tone blue crinkle finished metal toy. Features are: battery operated, on/off switch, foot pedal, tension and stitch length regulator, and extension table (not shown). "Made in Japan" is stamped on the sewing plate. 6½"h x 4"d x 8"w.

Plate 342. "SEW-ETTE" is written in metal script letters. The white top and handwheel are plastic, and the rest is blue crinkle finished metal. Features include: battery operated, foot pedal, tension and stitch length regulator. "Made in Japan" is stamped on the sewing plate. 6½"h x 5"d x 8½"w.

Plate 343. "SEW-ETTE" is written in yellow plastic script letters. The toy is metal with a red crinkle finish. Features include: battery operated, foot pedal (not shown), on/off switch, tension and stitch length regulator, and extension table (not shown). "Japan" is stamped on the sewing plate. 5¾"h x 4"d x 8"w.

Plate 344. "SEW-ETTE" is printed in raised letters on the upper arm. The metal toy has a black crinkle finish, and is mounted on a wood base. "Japan" is stamped on the sewing plate. It is battery operated with foot pedal and on/off switch. 6"h x 4¼"d x 8½"w.

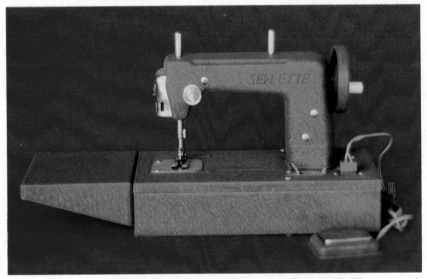

Plate 345. "SEW-ETTE" is printed in raised letters on the dark gray crinkle finished metal. Features are: battery operated, foot pedal, on/off switch, and extension table. "Japan" is stamped on the sewing plate. Toy from the collection of Wanda Wilson. 6"h x 4¼"d x 12½"w (includes extension table).

Sew E-Z

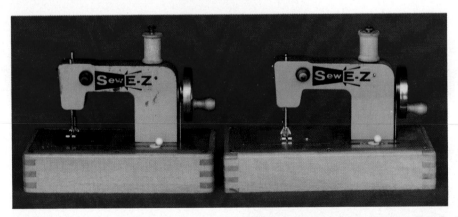

Plate 346. The two SEW E-Z toy machines appear to be the same, but one is larger. "Made in Berlin, Germany, US Zone" is stamped on the sewing plate. They are battery operated with on/off switch. The paint is a shiny metallic beige. Left: 6"h x 4¼"d x 7¾"w; right: 6"h x 4¾"d x 8½"w.

Plate 347. This SEW E-Z is finished in bright red shiny paint. "Made in Berlin, Germany, US Zone" is stamped on the sewing plate. It is battery operated. Toy from collection of Glenda Scott. 6"h x 4½"d x 8"w.

SEWMATE

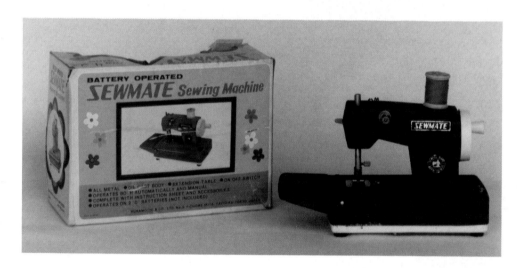

Plate 348. This small SEWMATE, K-1201 is dark gray metal with crinkle finish. The box has the "C. K." trademark with a diamond shape around it, and says "made in Japan." KURAMOCHI & CO. LTD. No. 3. 1-CHROME IRIYA, TAITO-KU TOKYO, JAPAN is the company listed on the box. The toy is battery operated with an on/off switch, and has an extension table (1 ¾" x 3¾"). 5½"h x 3¾"d x 6"w.

Plate 349. This small SEWMATE is bright shiny metal. The trademark "C. K." with a diamond shape around it and "Japan" are stamped on the bottom. It is battery operated with an on/off switch and extension table (1¾" x 3¾"). 5"h x 3¾"d x 6"w.

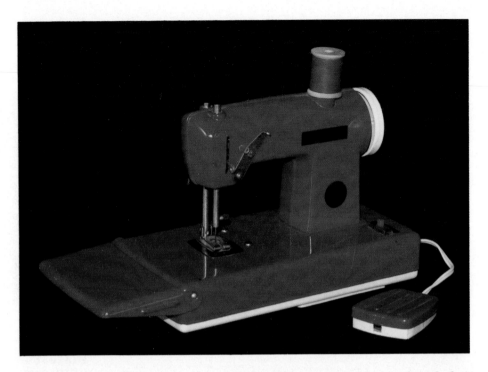

Plate 350. This shiny red metal SEWMATE is battery operated with foot pedal and on/off switch. The trademark CK with diamond shape around it is stamped on the bottom. Made in Japan. 6½"h x 4"d x 8"w.

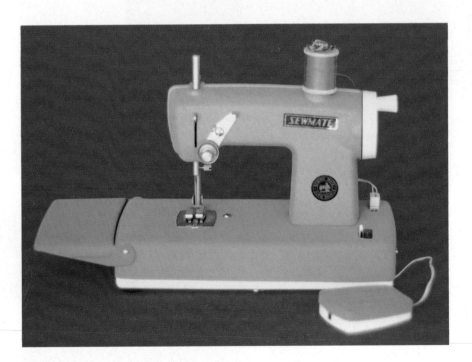

Plate 351. This SEWMATE is metal with a blue crinkle finish. The "CK" trademark with diamond shape around it and "Japan" are stamped on the bottom. Features are: battery operated, foot pedal, on/off switch, tension regulator, and extension table (2½" x 4"). 6½"h x 4"d x 8"w.

Plate 352 and 352A. The emblem on this toy says SEWING MACHINE instead of SewMate, but the design is the same. The metal machine with plastic base was available in several colors. Features are: battery operated, foot pedal, on/off switch, light, and extension table (not shown). The spool pin is located on the back side. "Made in Japan" is stamped on the bottom. 5"h x 3¾"d x 6"w.

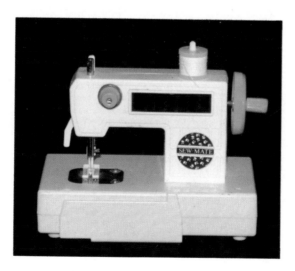

Plate 353. This SEWMATE is an entirely different style. "Made in Hong Kong No. 7822/7907" is stamped on the bottom. An extension table (3" x 3") folds under for storage. It is battery operated with foot pedal (not shown) and light. 6"h x 4"d x 6¾"w.

Singer Manufacturing Company

This company was founded by Isaac Merritt Singer and produced many sewing machines. Are these small Singer machines toys or portable machines for adults? This is the question asked because numerous boxes state, "Not a Toy." Several issues of *St. Nicholas Magazine* in the 1920s carried advertisements about these machines. The ads state, "Not a toy, if you are more than four years old, you can have your own sewing machine and easily learn to do work you will be proud to show to your friends." Often machines were advertised as a toy at Christmas time, and at other times of the year, they were advertised for adults. The adult advertisements say, "easily packed in a lady's traveling bag or suitcase and is therefore handy when traveling and convenient for vacation use." The 1953 instruction booklet says, "Not a toy...using this machine you will learn the basic principles of machine sewing, first making your dolly's clothes. You'll want to take your machine with you on vacations, weekend visits, and finally to college." Many boxes show a small girl sewing. Any mention of a child is reason to place them in the toy category. "Not a Toy" is intended as a sign of quality.

During the early years, the machines were made of heavy cast metal. The 1950s models were made of a lighter metal. Many are still available today and function well, attesting to the superb quality. They are very popular with collectors. The most recent models are made of plastic. If you think you have Singer duplicates, look carefully at all features. After close examination, you may find they are slightly different, probably indicating they were made a different year or manufactured in another country. Many of the instruction sheets were used for several years before being revised. SIMANCO (an abbreviation for Singer Manufacturing Co.) is written on many of the machines.

Britains Petite, Ltd. purchased the tools from Singer (France) in about 1980-81, and produced plastic machines (including their brand Petite) in Nottingham, England. This company is a licensee of Singer, authorized to retail Singer toy machines that are made in China. The DABS Co., West Islip, New York, is part of this company.

Information concerning Britains Petite furnished by Singer Sewing Co., Edison, New Jersey and Britains Petite, Nottingham, England.

If you are interested in a detailed history of the Singer Company and the founder, you should read "*A Capitalistic Romance—Singer and the Sewing Machine*" by Ruth Brandon. It is an excellent biography about the famous inventor.

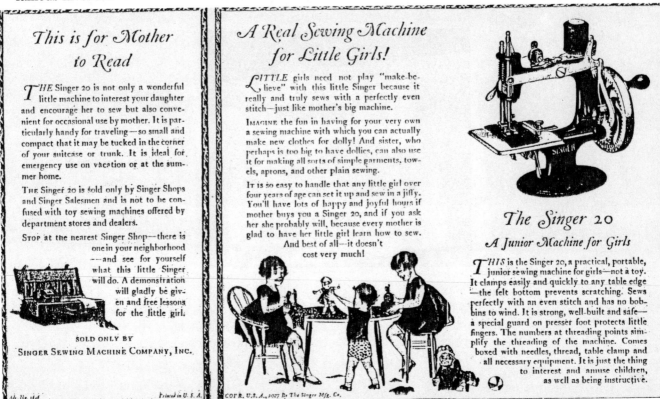

1927

The best way to date Singer toy sewing machines is by the instruction sheets. The copyright dates will be listed. Since most of these have been lost; the handwheels, bases, and boxes give clues to the date.

Left: 1910 – Nickel plated handwheel with cross bars. Middle: 1914 – Nickel plated spiral handwheel. Right: 1922 – Black spiral handwheel with nickel plated rim and arrows. Photograph courtesy of Marjorie Abel.

Left: Box for 1910 Model. Middle: Box for 1914 Model. Right: Box for 1922 Model. Since the 1914 and 1922 boxes are the same, you would need the instruction sheet for dating, or study all the features of these models when pictured later. All three boxes say: "As the twig is bent, the tree's inclined. This is not a toy, but a real Sewing Machine. Practical, Instructive, Useful, and Amusing." Photograph courtesy of Marjorie Abel.

Plate 354. The machine in the photograph was purchased without an instruction sheet, however "Singer Model No. 20 and Reissue November 15, 1910, is written on an instruction sheet with the same features and wheel design. This is a single thread sewing machine making an elastic chain stitch that does not ravel if the seam is locked as directed. For comparison with other models, these features should be noted: made of cast metal, there is no felt on the bottom of the oval base, the thread routes are not numbered on the machine, it has a stitch length regulator, but no tension regulator, and came with a table clamp. A gold Singer trademark emblem is painted on the back side. Thousands were manufactured in Elizabeth, New Jersey. Manufacturing information furnished by Singer Company, Edison, New Jersey. 6¼"h x 3"d x 7"w; c. 1910.

Plate 355. The features of the 1914 SINGER Model No 20 are: made of cast metal with oval base that has no felt on bottom, gear driven nickel plated spiral handwheel without arrows, wooden handle, tension and stitch length regulator, seam gauge, and table clamp. The instruction sheet shows a diagram of the thread routing, and the thread route is not numbered on the machine. A tension regulator has been added to this machine that was not on the 1910 model. The gold Singer emblem is painted on the back side. 6¼"h x 3"d x 7"w; c. 1914.

Plate 356. Features of the 1922 SINGER Model No. 20 are: made of cast metal with oval base that has felt covered pad on bottom, geared spiral handwheel that is black with nickel plated rim and arrows showing direction to turn wooden handle, tension and stitch length regulator, seam gauge, table clamp, and sews a chain stitch. The thread route is not numbered on the machine. The gold Singer emblem is painted on the back side. 6¼"h x 3"d x 7"w; c. 1922.

Plate 357. The next SINGER Model No. 20 was available in slight variations through the 1920s and 1930s. A feature added is the numbering of the thread route on the machine. Notice above the tension, there is a small raised numbering plate with number 4 written on it. Other features are: made of cast metal with oval felt covered base, spiral geared handwheel is black with a nickel plated rim and arrows, tension and stitch length regulators, seam gauge, table clamp, sews a chain stitch, and has gold Singer emblem painted on back side. 6¼"h x 3"d x 7"w; c. 1920s and 1930s.

Plate 358. The lettering on this SINGER is written in script. This box has "Made in USA" printed underneath the picture. Photograph courtesy of James and Sandra Seymour. 6¼"h x 3¾"d x 6¾"w; c. 1920s.

Plate 359. This Model Number 20 is photographed from the backside to show the USA written under the Singer gold emblem. All other features are identical to the photograph in Plate 357: numbered thread route with tiny raised plate above the tension with number 4 written on it, made of cast metal with felt covered oval base, black spiral handwheel with nickel rim and arrows, tension regulator, stitch length regulator, and seam gauge. 6¼"h x 3"d x 7"w; c. 1920s and 1930s.

Plate 360 and 360A. The MINI-SEWING MACHINE Model K-20 is a handcrafted reproduction of the original design that was first introduced in the 1920s. Information on the box says: "One of the earliest fully functional children's toys with a serious purpose in mind." It comes complete with cast-iron table clamp, the 1926 revised version of the user's manual, and spare needles pack. "Made in Turkey" is painted in gold letters on the back side. This reproduction toy has the USA printed below the Singer emblem and has all the features shown on the machine in the previous photograph. A wood dome cover was also available. 6¼"h x 3"d x 7"w; c. 1989 and 1990s.

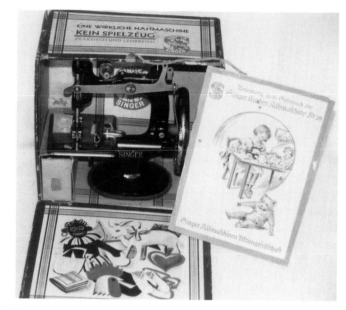

Plate 361. SINGER Model 20 was available in Germany. The famous Singer "S" on the instruction booklet and box has "Nahmaschine" (sewing machine) written on it. English translation of the German on the box is "A real machine, not a toy." Photograph courtesy of Judy Arnold. c. 1920s and 1930s.

Plate 362. SINGER Model 20-2 electric sewing machine was made especially for children. It is used only on 110 volt, 60 cycle, alternating current (A.C.). Two sewing speeds are provided, a slower speed for careful work, or for young children, and a faster speed for ordinary straight work. USA copyright dates on the instructions are 1922, 1926, and 1938. Photograph courtesy of Robert Brucato. 7"h x 6¼"d (includes motor) x 7"w; c. 1938.

Plate 363. SINGER Model 20-10 is often referred to as the "transition model," meaning that the features changed. Notice that the base is now rectangular, not oval. The spiral handwheel is painted a solid black. Other features include: made of cast metal, stitch and tension regulators, seam gauge, table clamp, and sews a chain stitch. The instruction sheet has copyright dates USA 1922, 1936, and 1948. Photograph courtesy of Cheryl Lansdown. 6½"h x 3½d" x 7"w; c. 1948 or later.

Plate 364. SINGER Sewing Machine Model 20-10 was available with complete mannikin set. The set includes: toy sewing machine, 2 Butterick patterns for doll clothes, clamp, instructions, and 11" high doll. Instructions show copyright dates USA 1922, 1936, 1948. A sewing handbook that accompanied this machine has a copyright date of 1949. Photograph courtesy of Robert Brucato. 6½"h x 3½"d x 7"w; c. 1949.

Plate 365 and 365A. The one hundred year "ANNIVERSARY" Singer is one of the most desirable models. "1851 to 1951" and "A century of Sewing Service" are written on the gold Singer emblem which is outlined in blue. The cast-metal toy has a gear driven black spiral handwheel and nickel plated sewing plate. Other features are: rectangular base, tension and stitch regulator, seam gauge, table clamp, numbered thread route, and sews a chain stitch. The market value is usually higher on this model than other 1950s models. 6½"h x 3½"d x 7"w; c. 1951.

Plate 366. SINGER SEWHANDY MANNIKIN SET with the anniversary model Singer (1851-1951) toy sewing machine came with the following: cast metal toy sewing machine, instruction booklet, clamp, needles, needle threader, sewing handbook, two Butterick patterns, and mannikin. Also a slot is for thimble and scissors which is missing from this set. Photograph courtesy of Ginny Meinig. 6½"h x 3½"d x 7"w; c. 1951.

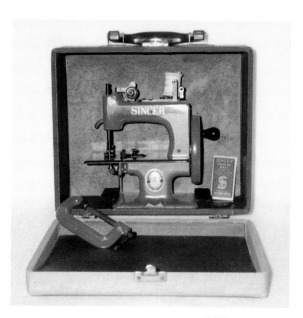

Plate 367 and 367A. The red and blue SINGER SEWHANDY are the most desirable Singer models sought by collectors. Very few collectors own these, so it is apparent that few were manufactured. A pale green model was also manufactured (not shown). The gold Singer emblem is on the front and Singer is printed on the front and back side. Photograph of two machines courtesy of Joseph and Louisa Llull. Photograph of machine and case courtesy of Marjorie Abel. 6½"h x 3½"d x 7"w; c. 1950s.

Plate 368 and 368A. The gold Singer emblem is outlined in black on this SINGER SEWHANDY Model 20. The machine has a flat beige crinkle paint finish. Sewing plate and gear driven spiral handwheel, are also painted. Other features are: made of cast metal, wheel has black handle, rectangular base, numbered thread route, tension and stitch length regulator, seam gauge, table clamp, hard carrying case, and sews a chain stitch. 6½"h x 3½"d x 7"w; c.1950s.

Plate 369. "Copyright USA 1953" is written on the instruction booklet of this SINGER SEWHANDY Model 20. The handwheel is also painted with the shiny black finish and has black arrows. Sewing plate is nickel plated. Other features are: made of cast metal, table clamp, stitch length and tension regulator, seam gauge, numbered thread route, table clamp, and sews a chain stitch. 6½"h x 3½"d x 7"w; c. 1950s.

Plate 370 and 370A. The gold Singer emblem is outlined in black on this Singer SEWHANDY Model 20. Features are: made of cast metal with shiny black finish, nickel plated sewing plate, gear driven black spiral handwheel with black arrows, presser foot is painted black, seam gauge, stitch length and tension regulator, thread route numbered, and sews a chain stitch.6½"h x 3½"d x 7"w; c. 1950s.

Plate 371. All features on the Singer Sewhandy Model 20 are identical to the previous photograph, except SINGER is printed in much smaller letters and the presser foot is nickel plated. 6½"h x 3½"d x 7"w; c. 1950s.

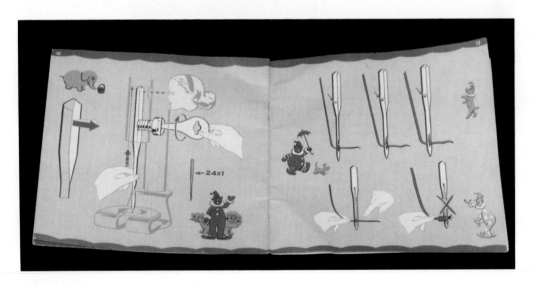

Plate 372 and 372A. An unusual instruction booklet accompanied this SINGER 20 SEWHANDY. It contains no writing, only clever illustrations with clowns and animals that could be understood in any language. "Copyright 1955" is printed inside. The style of handwheel has changed to solid construction and has "SIMANCO 29976" stamped on it. The machine, handwheel, and sewing plate are all painted shiny beige. Singer's famous "S" is shown on the gold emblem. Other features are: brown wooden handle on wheel, made of cast metal, table clamp, seam gauge, tension and stitch length regulator, numbered thread route, and sews a chain stitch. "Made in Great Britain" is written above the emblem. 6½"h x 3½"d x 7"w; c. 1950s.

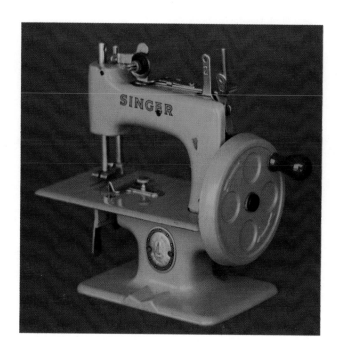

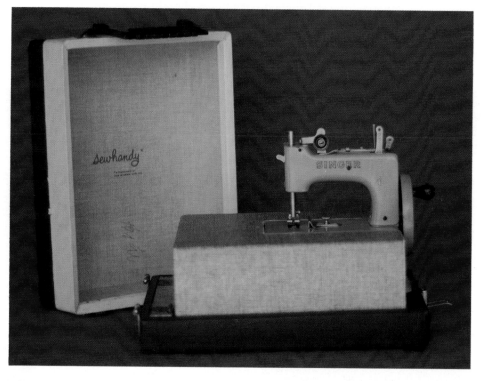

Plate 373 and 373A. "Made in Great Britain" is written above the gold Singer emblem. The machine, handwheel, and sewing plate are all painted shiny beige. The gear driven handwheel is of solid construction. A hard carrying case opens and folds out to make a very handy sewing table, however, it also came with a table clamp so it could be used elsewhere. Other features are: made of cast metal, handwheel has brown wooden handle, seam gauge, stitch length and tension regulator, thread route is numbered, and sews a chain stitch. 6½"h x 3½"d x 7"w; c. 1950s.

Plate 374 and 374A. This SINGER SEWHANDY Model 20 has a solid geared handwheel with "SIMANCO USA 29976" stamped on it. The machine is finished with beige crinkle paint, but the handwheel and sewing plate are painted shiny beige, and the wheel has a black handle. Other features are: made of cast metal, has table clamp, seam gauge, tension and stitch length regulator, numbered thread route, and sews a chain stitch. 6½"h x 3½"d x 7"w; c. 1950s.

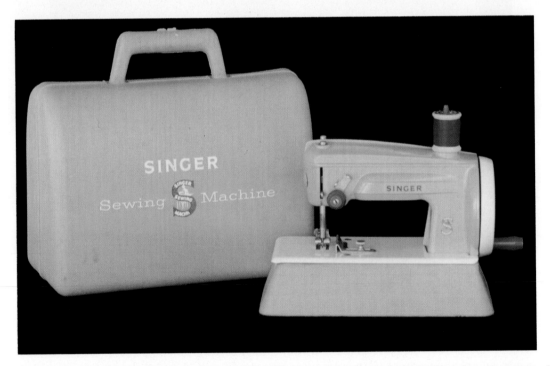

Plate 375. SINGER SEWHANDY Model 40K is made of cast metal. It is hand operated with a cog belt operating the bottom mechanism. "The Singer Manufacturing Co." and "Made in Great Britain" are written on the end of the base under the handwheel. All parts underneath have a number. The plastic carrying case is shaped like an old fashioned doctor's bag. The famous Singer "S" is shown on the case. 6¾"h x 4½"d x 8¾"w.

Plate 376. This little plastic Singer does not sew. Instead of a needle, it has a tiny blade for cutting (perhaps for patterns and etc.). The red Singer "S" is on the front and "The Singer Manufacturing Co., Made in USA Patent Pending" is written on the back. Suction feet are on the base for securing to the work surface. 5"h x 4¼"d x 6½"w.

Plate 377 and 377A. SINGER SEWHANDY Model 50 D is electric (A/C 110-120 volt). It has an on/off motor switch and a sew and stop lever. Other features are tension regulator and seam gauge. "Great Britain" is written on the back side. A plastic carrying case came with the machine. Montgomery Ward Christmas Catalog of 1964, offered this toy. 7¼"h x 5½"d x 11"w; c. 1960s.

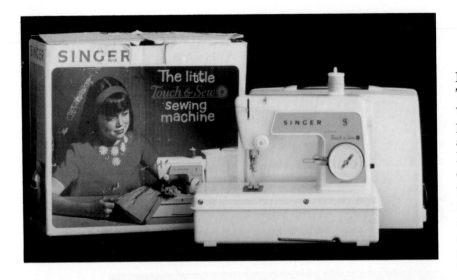

Plate 378. SINGER LITTLE TOUCH AND SEW, Model 67A, was available in several colors. A plastic snap on cover with handle accompanied the plastic machine. It was also available on a plastic convertible desk. The toy is battery operated or can be used with an electric adapter. It has an on/off power switch. Tiny fingers are protected from the needle by a specially designed presser foot. The machine has a bobbin and will sew a lockstitch. A small crank was available to attach to the wheel on the front for manual operation. A table clamp is attached to the machine. "Made in USA" is written on the front under the wheel. Yellow toy from collection of Glenda Scott. 9"h x 4½"d x 10"w; c. 1960s and 1970s.

Plate 378A. This is model 67A SINGER TOUCH AND SEW shown in blue.

Plate 378B. This is model 67A SINGER TOUCH AND SEW shown in gold.

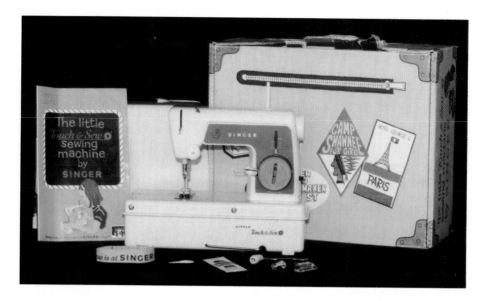

Plate 378C. Model 67A. SINGER TOUCH AND SEW is shown with box, case, and all accessories. Toy owned by Cathy Jones.

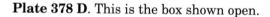

Plate 378 D. This is the box shown open.

Plate 379. SINGER JUNIOR MISS, Model 67B, is a battery operated toy with a foot pedal. It can also be used with an electric adapter. A hand crank can be inserted in the wheel to be used manually without a battery. Arrows indicate the direction to turn the wheel. The table clamp is attached to the machine. This toy has a bobbin and sews a lock-stitch. "Made in France" is written on the bottom. 9"h x 4½"d x 10"w; c. 1970s.

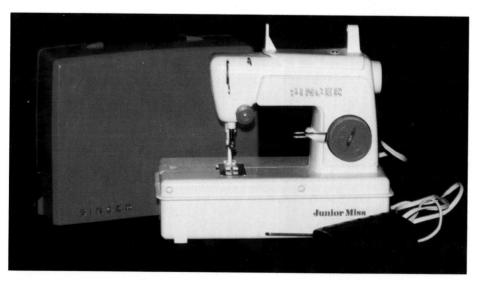

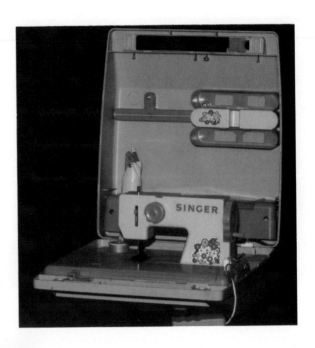

Plate 380. Many compartments and drawers for sewing accessories are built into the carrying case of this Singer toy center. The battery operated high-impact plastic machine folds up and latches inside the case to make a sewing table. The toy has a light and foot pedal. Small battery operated scissors were among the accessories. The 1982 Montgomery Ward Christmas Catalog sold this toy for $36.99. 3¾"h x 1½"d x 7½"w; c. 1980s. Case is 12" tall when closed.

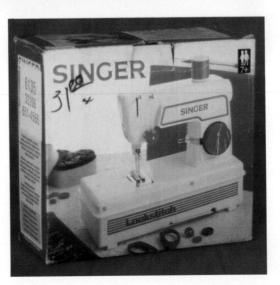

Plate 381 and 381A. Singer LOCKSTITCH has a bright red plastic carrying case. The plastic and metal toy is battery operated or can be used with an electric adapter. Features are: bobbin, foot pedal, adjustable tension dial, hand crank for manual control, attached table clamp. "Made in England" and "Model No. T 6406" are written on the bottom of the box. J. C. Penney Christmas Catalogs of 1987 to 1990 offered this machine for $36.99. 8½"h x 4½"d x 10"w; c. 1980s and 1990s.

Plate 382. The CHAINSTITCH Singer is battery operated with a foot pedal. The battery cover on the bottom of the machine in the photograph is missing. The thread spool is inside a small plastic cover on the top. This toy was made in England. 6"h x 4¾"d x 8"w; c. 1980s.

Plate 383. This Singer is also a CHAINSTITCH model. The plastic toy is battery operated with a foot pedal that has an on/off switch. The pedal is stored underneath the handwheel. A clear plastic compartment on top holds the thread. The instruction sheet is written in several languages: English, French, Italian, German, and Dutch. "Made in England" is written on the box. 6"h x 4¾"d x 8"w; c. 1980s.

Plate 384. This black and gold plastic CHAINSTITCH Singer model is battery operated with a foot pedal, or can be operated by hand. The box says not suitable for under 36 months. It was made in China and distributed by Britains Petite, Ltd. The J. C. Penney Christmas Catalogs of 1991 and 1992 offered this toy for $19.99. 6½"h x 4½"d x 9¼"w; c. 1990s.

Plate 385. Features of this plastic CHAINSTITCH Singer toy are: battery operated, working light, tension dial, on/off switch, foot pedal, carrying handle, storage compartment, and the thread spool is concealed in a compartment on top. It was made in China and distributed by Britains Petite, Ltd. and was featured in their 1993 catalog. 6½"h x 4½"d x 9¼"w; c. 1990s.

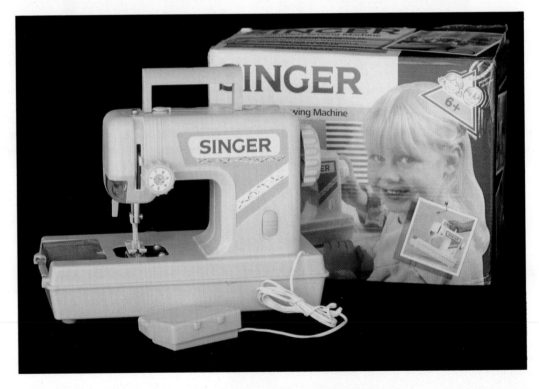

Plate 386. The pink and blue plastic Singer CHAINSTITCH is hand or battery operated. Features are: foot pedal, on/off switch, spool compartment on top, carrying handle, light, storage compartment, and tension dial. This toy is recommended for ages six and up. It was made in China and distributed by Britains Petite, Ltd. The J. C. Penney Christmas Catalog of 1993, offered this for $19.99. 6½"h x 4½"d x 9¼"w; c. 1990s.

Plate 387. The features of this Singer LOCKSTITCH are: foot pedal control, control indicator lights, battery operated, fast/slow speed control, stitch length regulator, working light, on/off switch, tension dial, circular bobbin and winder, free arm, carrying handle, and storage compartment. The toy can also be operated by an electric A/C adapter. It was made in China and distributed by Britains Petite, Ltd., and is featured in their 1993 catalog. Also the J. C. Penney Christmas Catalogs of 1991, 1992, and 1993, offered this toy for $44.99. 8½"h x 4½"d x 11¼"w; c. 1990s.

Plate 388. The SINGER TINY TAYLOR MENDING MACHINE, Model M100A, is often mistaken for a toy. It is an adult sewing machine made specifically for mending purposes. It was manufactured in the early 1980s in Canada. The machine is electric, has a bobbin, and sews a lock stitch. Information furnished by the Singer Company. 7"h x 4¾"d x 10¼"w; c. 1980s.

Plate 389. The SINGER FEATHERWEIGHT is a very popular sewing machine. It is definitely not a toy, but a small portable that weights only 11 pounds. Many seamstresses still use it, especially quilters. The machine is all metal. If you desire an in depth study of this machine, you should read the booklet "Featherweight 221. The Perfect Portable" by Nancy Johnson-Srebro, Silver Star Publishing. It gives a complete history and information on dating the machine. 10"h x 6¾"d x 10"w; extension table: 5½" x 6¾"; c. 1930 through 1950s.

Smith & Egge Manufacturing Company
Bridgeport, Connecticut

This firm was organized in the spring of 1874, and incorporated in September 1877. Friend William Smith was president and Frederick Egge was superintendent. They invented a lock and key for letter boxes and became successful bidders for government contracts, and for approximately 20 years made all the locks, keys, and chains for the US Postal Service. A specialty lock was also sold to the U. S. Treasury Department. Their catalog listed many hardware items, however, sash chains, punches, and locks are the items they were most noted for. Besides these and other lines, they manufactured sewing machine hardware for Singer, Wheeler & Wilson, Domestic, Estey Organ, and other companies, and also made the universal button hole attachment.

Mr. Egge had a reputation of being one of the best and most ingenious mechanics in the country. Mr. Smith was a very active republican, and was appointed Postmaster of Bridgeport under President Lincoln for 8 years before establishing Smith & Egge Manufacturing Co. In 1891, Mr. Smith organized Automatic Chain Co. of Birmingham, England. He also organized the Bridgeport Deoxidized Bronze and Metal Co. and Lake Torpedo Boat Co. F. W. Smith died March 3, 1917, at age 88.

Information furnished by Robert Brucato. His information obtained from *The History of Bridgeport & Vacinity* by S. J. Clark Publishing Co. of 1917, and *History of City of Bridgeport, Connecticut* by Rev. Samuel Orcutt, published under the auspices of the Fairfield County Historical Society.

This is another brand with the question: Is this a toy or adult machine? An old advertisement for Smith and Egge Automatic says: "This is not a toy, weighs 2½ pounds, can be packed in corner of trunk, simple enough for a child to operate." Macy's Christmas Gift Catalog of 1906, shows a Smith and Egge Automatic under the title "Special Values in Girl's Toys."

Plate 390. "SMITH AND EGGE AUTOMATIC 1901" is stamped on a plate attached to the front of this tiny cast-iron sewing machine. It has a hand crank instead of a wheel, has automatic tension, stitch length regulator, and sews a chain stitch. Photograph courtesy of Marjorie Abel. 6¾"h x 6"w; c. 1901.

Plate 391."SMITH & EGGE AUTOMATIC" is stamped on a textured plate attached to the front of this machine. Note that it is operated by a hand crank that is chain driven. The seam or cloth gauge is missing from the sewing plate on the machine in the photograph. Features are: automatic tension, stitch length regulator, and sews a chain stitch. Photograph courtesy of Marjorie Abel. 7⅛"h x 6"w; c. early 1900s.

Plate 392. "AUTOMATIC" is written in raised letters on the front of this tiny cast-iron Smith and Egge machine. Features are: automatic tension, stitch length regulator, hand crank, and sews a chain stitch. 6½"h x 6"w; c. early 1900s.

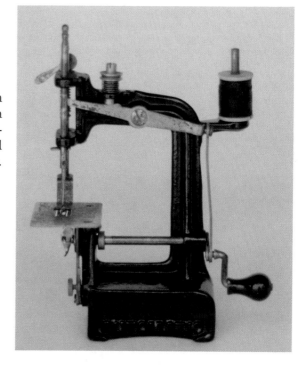

Plate 393."PEERLESS AUTOMATIC" is written in raised letters on the front of this tiny cast-iron Smith and Egge machine. "Pat. June 2, 96, Jan 26, 97, and Oct 19, 97" is stamped on the sewing plate. The instruction sheet says it can be used for embroidering by stamping the design on the under side, and the embroidery stitch will then appear on the right side when sewed. Features are: hand crank, stitch length regulator, automatic tension, and sews a chain stitch. It was packed in a plain wooden box. 6½"h x 6"w; c. 1897 and early 1900s.

Plate 394. "THE LITTLE COMFORT" is written on a plate attached to the front of this Smith and Egge. Features of this tiny cast-iron machine are: chain drive, automatic tension, stitch length regulator, has cloth or seam gauge, and sews a chain stitch. Photograph courtesy of Marjorie Abel. 7½"h x 6½"w; c. early 1900s.

Plate 395. "LITTLE COMFORT IMPROVED" is written on the front edge of the sewing plate of this Smith and Egge model. An old advertisement shows that the original selling price was $4.00. This machine operates with a gear driven handwheel, not a hand crank. Note the unusual thread pin. Push it backward and the empty spool will drop off. Insert a new one and turn back. Other features are: table clamp, seam gauge, stitch length regulator, automatic tension, and sews a chain stitch. Wilcox and Gibbs needles were used. Photograph courtesy of Robert Brucato. 7"h x 6½"w; c. early 1900s.

Plate 396. "LITTLE COMFORT IMPROVED" is written on the front edge of the sewing plate of this inverted C shaped machine. A geared handwheel is used with this Smith & Egge model. Features include: stitch length regulator, automatic tension, and table clamp. Photograph courtesy of Marjorie Abel. 7½"h x 7¼"w; c. early 1900s.

Sotoy

Plate 397 and 397A. MARTHA WASHINGTON SOTOY was manufactured by the Metallograph Corporation of New York, U. S. A. "Sotoy" is a trademark registered with the U. S. Patent Office. Martha Washington's picture appears on a metal plate that is attached to the front. A red metal plate attached to the back side gives all manufacturing information. This toy appeared in the Sears, Roebuck, and Co. Catalog in 1919. Original selling price was $2.87. It is made of sheet steel with a cast-iron wheel, and sews a chain stitch. 6½"h x 4½"d x 7¾"w; c. 1919.

Plate 398. Gold lettering on the back base says "Made by THE HAEUSERMANN METAL MFG. CO., New York U.S.A." "SOTOY" is written in big red letters on the front of this metal toy. Photograph courtesy of Marjorie Abel. 7"h x 4½"d x 8"w; c. pre WWII.

Spenser Sewing Machine Co.
208 Tremont Street,
Boston, Mass.

Plate 399. SPENCER, a cast-iron machine, has patent information written on the sewing plate: "Made in USA, Patented June 19, 1900, Feb. 19, 1901, Mar. 28, 1902, others pending." A *Harper Magazine* advertisement listed this as an "Automatic Hand Sewing Machine" with an introductory price of $10.00, with the following features: actual automatic tension, practically noiseless, ball bearing in important parts, a hardened feed and self-setting needle, and a large range of stitches. Photograph courtesy of Joseph and Louisa Llull. 9"h x 9"w; c. early 1900s.

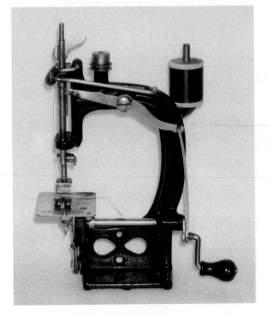

Plate 400. This SPENSER machine is made of cast iron. Features are: tension and stitch regulator, hand crank instead of wheel, and requires a table clamp. Another model very similar to this has a device that attaches to the machine. Using the device, you do not have to turn the wheel as often thus sewing faster. Photograph courtesy of Marjorie Abel. 6¾"h x 1½"d x 5⅞"w; c. early 1900s.

Steinfeldt & Blasberg
Hanover, Germany

Plate 401. The rare NUREMBERG PRINCESS (sometimes called the Nuremberg Lady) was patented by Max Sandt in 1891 in Germany, and in May 1892 in England. The manufacturer is Steinfeldt and Blasberg, Hanover. The toy is made of cast iron and has been found painted pink or blue. An advertisement of 1894 claims "Best present for a girl and a perfect chain stitch sewing machine in miniature, equally as strongly made, and producing as good sewing, as a full size machine." This is the most desirable toy sewing machine ever made, and is extremely rare. Only a few are known to exist. Since the company was only in business a few years, it is understandable that this machine is so rare. Photograph and information courtesy of Maggie Snell. 7½"h x 3"d x 7"w; c. 1890s.

Plate 402. The rare NUREMBERG CLOWN was patented by Max Sandt in 1891 in Germany and in 1892 in England and manufactured by Steinfeldt and Blasberg. The toy is made of cast iron. This is also one of the most desirable and rare toy sewing machines. Only a few are known to exist. Photograph and information courtesy of Maggie Snell. 7½"h x 3"d x 7"w; c. 1890s.

Straco

Plate 403. "JET SEW-O-MATIC, A STRA-CO MACHINE" is printed in gold letters on the front of the base. "Made in England" is stamped on the sewing plate. Features are: metal base, plastic body, spool pin and tension on the front base, manually operated, and sews a chain stitch. Distributed by F. J. Strauss Co., Inc., 1107 Broadway, New York, New York 10010. Note the zip code on the address indicates it was distributed after 1963. 6½"h x 4¾"d x 9"w; c. 1960s.

Plate 404. "JET SEW-O-MATIC, A Straco Machine" is written in gold letters on the front of the base. "Made in England" is stamped on the sewing plate. The toy has a metal base and plastic body and is hand operated. 7"h x 4¾"d x 9"w.

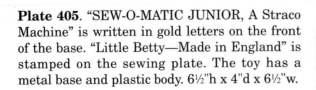

Plate 405. "SEW-O-MATIC JUNIOR, A Straco Machine" is written in gold letters on the front of the base. "Little Betty—Made in England" is stamped on the sewing plate. The toy has a metal base and plastic body. 6½"h x 4"d x 6½"w.

Plate 406. A STRACO decal is on the upper arm and "Made in England" is stamped on the sewing plate. Features are: metal base, plastic body, manually operated, and sews a chain stitch. 6½"h x 4"d x 6½"w.

Plate 407. "Made in England" is stamped on the sewing plate of this toy, but no other decals are on the plastic body. The base is metal. 6½"h x 4"d x 6½"w.

Plate 408. "SEW-O-MATIC SENIOR A Straco Machine" is printed on the front of the base. "Little Betty—Made in England" is stamped on the sewing plate. Features are: metal base, plastic body, hand operated, tension regulator, and sews a chain stitch. 6½"h x 5"d x 8½"w.

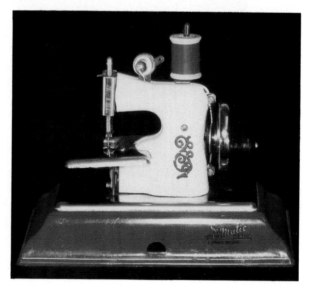

Plate 409. LB STRACO is plastic with a metal base. The hand operated toy sews a chain stitch. "Made in England" is engraved on the sewing plate. Photograph courtesy of Judy Arnold. 7"h x 4"d x 6½"w.

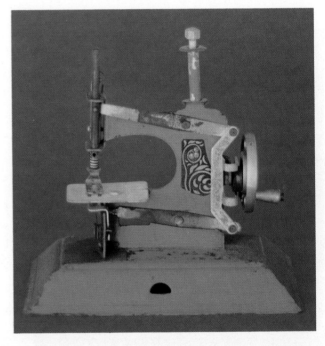

Plate 410. "Made in England" is stamped on the sewing plate of this toy. It has a single sheet metal body. Toy from collection of Wanda Wilson. 6"h x 4"d x 6½"w.

Plate 411. "LITTLE BETTY, A Straco Machine" is printed in gold letters on the front of the base. "Little Betty—Made in England" is stamped on the sewing plate. The toy has a single sheet metal body. Toy from collection of Wanda Wilson. 6"h x 4"d x 6½"w.

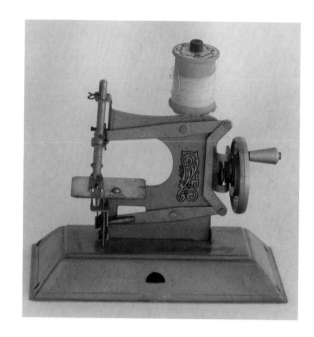

Plate 412. "LITTLE BETTY" is printed in gold letters on the top of the base. "Made in England" is stamped on the sewing plate. The toy has a single sheet metal body. Toy from collection of Glenda Scott. 6"h x 4"d x 6½"w.

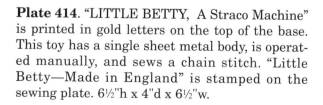

Plate 413. "LITTLE BETTY, A Straco Machine" is printed in gold letters on the front of the base. This toy has a metal base and plastic body, is operated manually, and sews a chain stitch. "Made in England" is stamped on the sewing plate. 6½"h x 4"d x 6½"w.

Plate 414. "LITTLE BETTY, A Straco Machine" is printed in gold letters on the top of the base. This toy has a single sheet metal body, is operated manually, and sews a chain stitch. "Little Betty—Made in England" is stamped on the sewing plate. 6½"h x 4"d x 6½"w.

Plate 415. STRACO ELECTRO SUPER JET SEW-O-MATIC was made in Japan. Many other Straco models have plastic heads, but this blue and white one is metal. The base is also metal. It is battery operated with on/off switch. Photograph courtesy of Joe and Evelyn Watkins. 5½"h x 5⅛"d x 8¾"w; c. 1950s and 1960s.

Plate 416. The red and white STRACO ELECTRO SUPER JET SEW-0-MATIC is battery operated, with an on/off switch. It is all metal and marked "Made in Japan." 6½"h x 5"d x 8½"w.

Plate 417. The STRACO ELECTR-O-MATIC toy is belt driven. Note the Casige emblem on the body, indicating it was made in Germany. Photograph courtesy of Conrad and Jo Ann Overton. 7½"h x 4¼"d x 8½"w; c. 1950s.

Plate 418. LITTLE BETTY is a chain stitch miniature sewing machine with a decal labeled DEBUTANTE. It is made of bright blue plastic with a gray base. The thread pin is on the right corner of the base, and is missing from the machine in the photograph. The white knob is the tension regulator. This toy was manufactured by E. M. Gheysens Ltd., Lorne Road, Dover, Kent, England. Photograph courtesy of Judy Arnold. 7½"h x 6¼"d x 12"w.

Tabitha

Plate 419. The TABITHA is tiny enough to fit in the palm of your hand, however, this is another machine with the question: Is this a toy or adult portable? No advertisements have surfaced stating it was intended as a toy. It is made of brass by the Manhattan Brass Co. in New York and sold by Daniel Johnson & Son from offices in New York and London. "The Tabitha — Pat Appld. For" is stamped in high relief on the base. Photograph courtesy of Estelle Zalkin. 3¾"h x 2½"d x 4¼"w; c. 1885.

Made in Taiwan
Republic of China

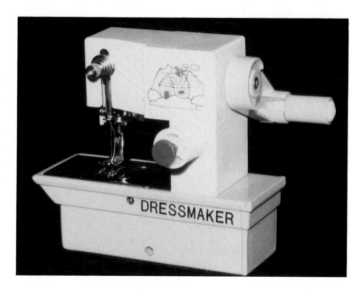

Plate 420. The DRESSMAKER mini sewing machine was distributed by Jenq Shenq Enterprise Co., Ltd., and manufactured in Taiwan. The patent number is 52681 and the model number is JS-90A. It is made of plastic and metal, available in pink or blue, and sews a chain stitch. A table clamp was furnished. 5¼"h x 1¼"d x 6¾"w; c. 1992.

Tomy

This is a Japanese owned company, the biggest toy company in Japan. All the research and development is done in Tokyo and manufactured by Tomy owned factories. Third party manufacturers are used for some products. Tomy was set up in the United Kingdom in the 1980s, and in 10 years has become one of that countries top five companies. Tomy America was a very strong company in the 1970s, but unfortunately the Tomy company had to sell to Coleco in the early 1980s due to the tough economic times. A few years later, Coleco went bankrupt, and this gave Tomy the opportunity to buy back the name in the USA. Gradually the market share is building back. Tomy America has been located in Brea, California, since 1991. Photographs are from the catalog "The Magical World at Tomy 1992/93." Information and catalog furnished by Tomy UK, Ltd., Wells House, 231 High St., Sutton, Surrey SMl 1LD, United Kingdom.

Plate 421. TOMY—SEW REAL, a battery powered toy, is recommended for ages 7 and up. It has a bobbin and works like an adult machine. c. 1990s.

Plate 422. TOMY—MY FIRST SEWING MACHINE is simple to operate. The battery powered chain stitch toy is recommended for ages 5 and up. c. 1990s

Tourist

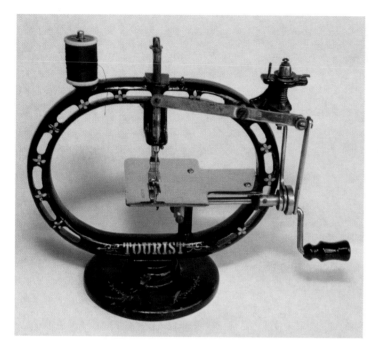

Plate 423. TOURIST was manufactured by the Stewart Manufacturing Co., (W. J. Stewart, Prop). The oval base is wood with a few gold scrolls across the front. The frame is cast iron and painted with delicate turquoise flowers with red centers. The Montgomery Ward Catalog's toy section featured this Tourist in 1903, with selling price of $2.95. This toy sewing machine is scarce, and it is unknown how many still exist. Photograph and information courtesy of Ginny Meinig. 8"h x 10½"w (including handle); c. 1903.

Triumph

Plate 424. The frame of the TRIUMPH toy sewing machine is made of wood with metal parts. It is elegantly enameled and finished in floral designs of different colors. The word "Patented" is on the sewing plate. It fastens to the table with a clamp. The Sears, Roebuck, and Co. Catalog of 1902, featured this toy for $1.25, and the Montgomery Ward Catalog of 1903, offered it for $1.50. The ad says "for the little miss, for the nursery maid, for all kinds of plain family sewing and is adapted largely for kindergarten use." This toy is relatively scarce. Photograph courtesy of Joseph and Louisa Llull. 7½"h x 7"w (including knob); c. early 1900s.

Made in USA

Plate 425. LILY is a small cast-iron toy with gilt decorations. It was probably made in the USA, but the manufacturer is unknown. Photograph and information courtesy of Maggie Snell. 5½"h x 2"d x 6½"w; c. late 1800s.

Plate 426. LITTLE GEM No. 6103 was distributed by Western Stamping Corp., 2203 W. Michigan Ave., Jackson, Michigan 49202. "US & Foreign Patents Pend., Made in USA" is printed on the bottom. The plastic toy is recommended for ages 6 and older. Toy from the collection of Glenda Scott. 6"h x 3½"d x 7¼"w.

Made in U.S.S.R.

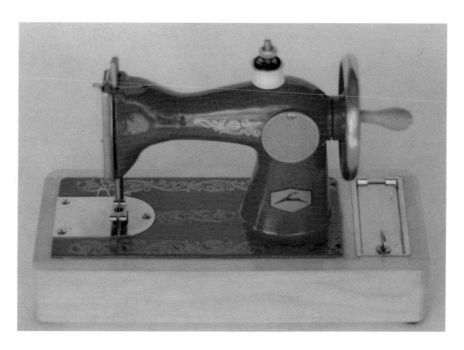

Plate 427. This sturdily built toy was made in USSR. The head is metal and mounted on a wood base that contains a small storage compartment. This model was available in various colors. A chain stitch is formed, and the tension regulator is on top of the spool pin. The instruction sheet is written in the Russian language. Part of the translation is: "This toy sewing machine is designed to develop sewing skills in preschool children and children between ages 6 to 9. This toy can perform embroidery and chain stitch." The instructions give complete directions how to sew and clean the toy, and how to tie off the stitch to keep it from raveling out. Address listed on the instructions is: 211030, Orsha, Vostochoi Pereulok, 17 Obedinenie, Promshveimash, USSR. 7"h x 4½"d x 10"w;c. 1980s. Russian translation by: Elena Austinova Anderson, assistant to the Professor at the history department, Midwestern State University, Wichita Falls, Texas.

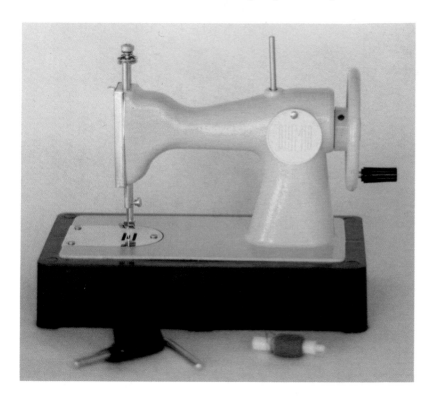

Plate 428. This sturdily built lime green toy was also made in USSR. The machine head is metal, but the base is black plastic. It is manually operated and sews a chain stitch, and came equipped with a table clamp and plastic thread spool. 7"h x 4½"d x 8½"w; c. 1980 and 1990s.

Vulcan

Plate 429. The VULCAN SENIOR is an elegant toy made of cast metal. "Made in England" is printed on the front. It has a free arm style, is manually operated, and sews a chain stitch. 7"h x 3¾"d x 8½"w.

Plate 430. VULCAN JUNIOR is a quality built hand operated metal toy. "Made in England" is written on the upper arm. The long narrow shape resembles a large stapler. Photograph courtesy of Joe and Evelyn Watkins. 6⅛"h x 3¼"d x 8"w; c. 1950s and 1960s.

Plate 431 and 431A. The VULCAN MINOR was made in England in 1963. The metal toy is manually operated and sews a chain stitch. Photograph courtesy of Cumberland Toy and Model Museum. 5½"h x 2¾"d x 6¼"w. c. 1960s.

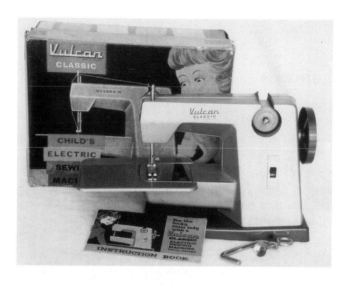

Plate 432. VULCAN CLASSIC is an all metal child's electric sewing machine. It is battery operated with an on/off switch. Features include a free arm with extended sewing plate. Photograph courtesy of Judy Arnold. 7¼"h x 4"d x 12½"w.

Plate 433. The VULCAN COUNTESS is the perfect name for this royal toy. It is made of cast metal and manually operated with a free arm style. The spool of thread is inserted in the front of the machine. "Made in England" is printed on the front. 7"h x 4¼"d x 9½"w.

VOGUE

Plate 434. This VULCAN toy is made of metal. Although parts of this machine are missing, it has been added here to point out the unusual oval plate on the middle of the base. It has a raised design of a spool of thread and needle. Toy from collection of Wanda Wilson. 6½"h x 4"d x 6"w.

Plate 435. "VOGUE SEWING MACHINE" is written on this black all metal toy. A small drawer for storing sewing accessories pulls out. The top flips back for easy access to the sewing mechanism. No other marks appear on the machine, however it is very similar to the "Junior Miss" machines made by Artcraft Metal Products Inc., West Haven, CT, only this machine is all metal and the "Junior Miss" has a wood base and no drawer. Photograph courtesy of Joseph and Louisa Llull. 7½"h x 10"w; c. 1940s and 1950s.

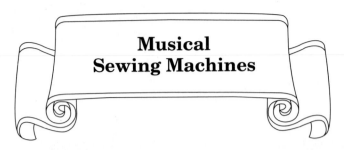

Musical Sewing Machines

The concept of a musical sewing machine is not new. A "Musical Sewing Machine Cover" for a treadle machine was offered as early as October 1882, by Garvie and Wood. When the treadle was pumped to activate the sewing machine, it also created music. Reference: *The Sewing Machine, Its Invention and Development* by Grace Rogers Cooper, published by the Smithsonian Institution Press.

Plate 436. The ELNA JUNIOR could be purchased with or without a music box. The song played by this model is the "Blue Danube Waltz." Manufactured in Switzerland. For complete manufacturing information see Plate 119. 7"h x 4"d x 9¼"w; c. 1956.

Plate 437. This beige and brown ELNA JUNIOR is a musical toy sewing machine. The music box can be turned on or off with a tiny switch on the front. A variety of songs was available. For complete manufacturing information, see plate 119. Photograph courtesy of Georg Reinfelder. 7"h x 4"d x 9¼"w; c. 1958.

Plate 438. This NECCHI, a fascinating green beauty, delighted many little girls. By turning the handwheel, a music box started and played as long as the machine sewed. The music could be turned off if the father sleeps, or the mother no longer wished to hear the music. Made in Italy. Photograph courtesy of Georg Reinfelder. 6¼"h x 4¼"d x 8¼"w; c.1955.

Plate 439. This charming musical addition to your sewing room will remind you to take time out for a "spot of tea." The tune is "Remember." This Item # 448990 is manufactured by Enesco Corporation, Elk Grove Village, IL 60193. Photograph and information courtesy of Enesco Corp. 9½"h; introduced in 1991.

Plate 440. SEW PETITE plays the tune "My Favorite Things." This enchanting, old-fashion sewing machine reproduction is animated with a needle that pulses up and down. The wheel spins 'round and 'round. A little boy mouse on the top skips rope with the thread while a little girl mouse pivots back and forth on a spool. Made in China exclusively for Enesco Corporation, Elk Grove Village, IL 60193. Item #569682. Photograph and information courtesy of Enesco Corporation. 7"h x 4½"d x 7½"w; c. 1989 to 1993.

Plate 441. HOMESPUN HOLIDAYS is a delightful musical accent. As the spool of thread revolves atop the machine, a fellow swings a thimble-full of lights to a crew below. The thread shuttle moves up and down on fabric, which is being stamped as it moves back and forth. The bobbin winder and handwheel revolve. A spool of thread spins around to tie up packages. Item # 592455. Manufactured by Enesco Corporation. Photograph and information courtesy of Enesco Corporation. 1993.

Plate 442. A RADIO TOY SEWING MACHINE should delight every little seamstress. The battery operated toy sews a chain stitch. Dials for stations and volume are on the left side, and the speakers are underneath. It is made of plastic and decorated with floral decals. Made in Japan. Photograph courtesy of Claire Toschi.

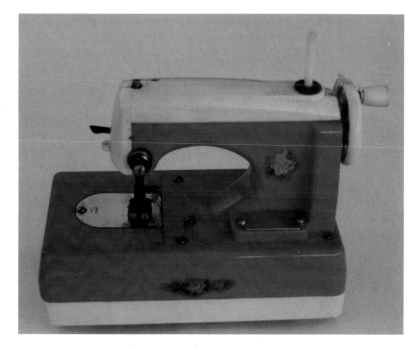

Plate 443. This copper sewing machine is a musical. It plays the tune "The Way We Were." The machine does not actually sew. Photograph courtesy of Claire Toschi. 8½"h x 3½"d x 7"w.

Plate 444. Turn the handwheel to wind the music box on this tin machine, and you will hear the tune "Second Hand Rose." A sticker on the bottom, says "Made in British Crown Colony Hong Kong." 6¾"h x 5"d x 9¼"w.

Plate 445. Spools of thread surround this miniature sewing machine. The music box is in the base and plays "Tara's Theme." A sticker on the base says "Enesco Musical, made in Taiwan." Base: 5¾"d x 7¾"w; machine: 4"h x 1½"d x 3⅜"w; c. 1990s.

Plate 446. "Home Sweet Home" is an appropriate song for this old fashioned treadle sewing machine. It reminds us of family traditions and patriotism. Made in China. Distributed by San Francisco Music Box Co. 3¼"h x 2"d x 3½"w; c. 1990s.

Plate 447. A kitten and sewing machine make a lovely combination for this porcelain musical that plays "Lara's Theme." It goes around and around as the music plays. Made in Taiwan. Distributed by San Francisco Music Box Co. 4"h x 3½"d x 3½"w; c. 1990s.

Plate 448. This musical sewing machine is cast of heavy cement type material. The machine does not sew and the drawers do not open, but it plays a delightful tune "Yesterday." Made in Taiwan and distributed by George Good Corp. 1988, City of Industry, California. Photograph courtesy of Claire Toschi. 4¾"h x 3"d x 4¾"w; c. 1988.

Plate 449. Press the bottom of this charming Christmas ornament and you will hear a holiday tune. Made in China. 2¼"h x 1½"d x 2¾"w; c. 1990s.

Plate 450. Hand-painted Mouse Pals will fill your hours with cheer as the tune "Do-Re-Me" is played. The large glass water dome sparkles with glitter. Made in Taiwan. Distributed by San Francisco Music Box Co. 6¼"h x 4"d x 4"w; c. 1990s.

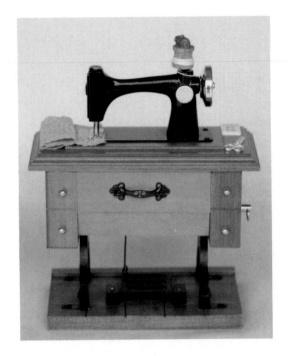

Plate 451. Wind up this sewing machine to hear it play "Buttons and Bows" as the treadle goes up and down and the spool revolves. Added details are scissors, E-Z pattern, fabric bolt, dozing mouse atop the revolving spool, and walnut finished wood table. "Berkeley Designs and Made in Taiwan" are printed on the bottom. This is available from many mail order catalogs and gift shops. 8¼"h x 4"d x 6⅞"w; c. 1990s.

Plate 452. "Yesterday" is the tune played by this wind up sewing machine. Made in Taiwan and distributed in 1978, by George Good Corp., City of Industry, California. 7"h x 3¾"d x 6½"w; c. 1978.

Plate 453. "Yesterday" is the tune played by this wind up sewing machine. This musical machine is almost identical to the one in the previous photograph, but the wood is different. Made in Taiwan and distributed in 1982, by George Good Corp., City of Industry, California. Machine owned by Sherry Strange. 7"h x 3¾"d x 6½"w; c. 1982.

Toy Treadles

It is the dream of all toy sewing machine collectors to add a toy treadle to their collection. A very prominent collector, Georg Reinfelder of Germany, specializes in toy treadles. Many of the photographs as well as the article below were furnished by him.

Toy treadles are the queens of toy sewing machines. Manufacturing dates began before the turn of the century until after WWI. Every little girl wished for one, but very few wishes came true. These toys were expensive and economic times were hard. Daily necessities came first, and little money was left for toys, especially such a high priced one.

The treadle was the most practical toy sewing machine for learning to sew. Other small lightweight hand models required the right hand to turn the wheel, leaving only the left hand for sewing. Often a family member would turn the wheel, leaving both hands free. Indeed using this toy required extreme skill which the small child had not achieved. This should have been fun, but in reality was very strenuous. The invention of the toy treadle using the foot pedal was the best resolution to this problem. Both hands were now free, and the young seamstress could sew just like her mother with her adult treadle. Owning this valuable toy made the girl proud and the envy of her friends, and was also socially prestigious for the parents.

Manufacturers produced very few toy treadles in comparison to the other toy sewing machines, and not many have survived. These are scarce and therefore very desirable to collectors. If you find one of these queens, the price is usually an unreasonable amount.

Very often the cast-iron stands are broken, or the toy has moisture damage from remaining in damp cellars for years. Wooden tables are no longer polished and metal has rusted. Important parts are frequently loose or missing. A major catastrophe for the collectors is to find a queen that has been repainted or has bad repairs.

An avid toy sewing machine collector found a beautiful queen in a tiny antique store. The price was very reasonable. Usually it takes more than one person to carry a treadle, but elated by the feeling of Christmas and excitement of this great find, the collector tried to manage all obstacles and carry this treasure alone. As the collector stumbled over an obstruction and fell, he awakened to find this was just a dream. He turned over in the bed, flipped on the light, and found no treadle in sight. Oh! What a misfortune! Nevertheless, it was a good dream, and very common among collectors. So, keep dreaming. One day, you may find your lucky star and awaken with a real toy treadle standing by your bed. Dream the treadle-vision!

Georg Reinfelder

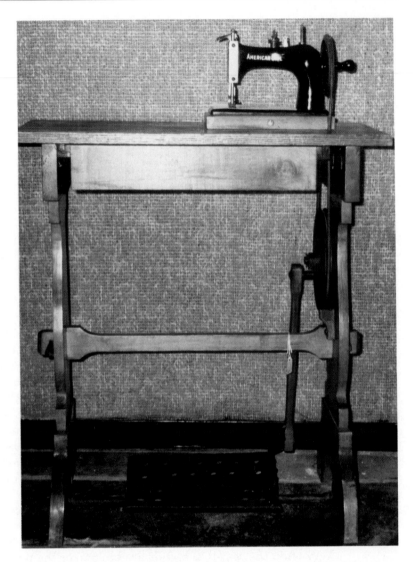

Plate 454. AMERICAN GIRL toy treadle was manufactured by National Sewing Machine Co. of Belevidere, Illinois, a prominent manufacturer of toy and adult sewing machines. The stand and table are wood. The foot pedal and drive wheel are cast iron. The machine head is almost identical to the hand model American Girl. Photograph courtesy of Louise Dwortachek. c. 1920s and 1930s.

Plate 455. LITTLE DAISY treadle has gold lettering on the center front of the frame that says: "TULLY'S PATENTED JULY 3, 1883." The cast-iron frame supports the wood table top which is 17¾" x 10". On each side of the frame is gold vertical stenciling with a gold daisy that has a green stem and leaves with the name "LITTLE DAISY" below. The sewing plate is 3¾" x 2⅛" and on it is printed "DAISY SMCO, CLEVELAND O, USA, PATENTED JULY 3, 1883, No 2562." The head of the machine is black with a gold stenciled design on the base. A fancy bonnet that matches the table top fits over the head. Under the table top on the left side is a drawer that swings out sideways. Photograph courtesy of Ginny Meinig. c. 1883.

Plate 456. LITTLE TOT toy treadle has the following inscription on the sewing plate: "Daisy Tot Mfg. Co. Albany, N.Y. approved Little Tot, Patented July 6, 1888." The machine head, treadle base, foot pedal, and drive wheel are cast iron. The table top is very simple with no drawers. The words "LITTLE TOT" are marked on the treadle base in the middle and on both sides. Photograph courtesy of Joseph and Louisa Llull. c. 1888.

Plate 457. The IDEAL treadle has a splendid and ornate foot pedal. The base is completely cast iron, and the sides have an insert that is lettered "IDEAL." Older and younger girls can use this treadle very comfortably by adjusting the foot pedal in a higher or lower position. This toy was advertised in the *Youth's Companion Magazine* December 19, 1895. The ad says: "The Ideal is the only practicable sewing machine for girls, a machine for mother's work, and the daughter's amusement and education. Distributed by Peck and Snyder, 130 Nassau Street, NY City." Another ad appeared in the *Ladies Home Journal* in 1895, with distributor Domestic Engineering Co. and Marshal Field and Co. as wholesale agent. Photograph courtesy of Georg Reinfelder. Magazine advertisements furnished by Marjorie Abel. c. 1895.

Plate 458. MÜLLER treadle, model 16, is the most elegant of the Müller treadles. The foot pedal has the casting letter "M," and is the only signature on this rare toy sewing machine. Photograph and information courtesy of Georg Reinfelder. c. 1920s.

Plate 459. The sisters, MÜLLER models 21, 18, 16 (left to right) were born between the great wars, and are eagerly sought by collectors. All three treadles are the same height above the floor: 26¾" to the wooden working table. These treadles use the same models as the Müller hand driven toy sewing machines. Treadle 16 is the model 15 with another base. Treadle 18 is the heavy model 12. Treadle 21 is the model 19, but without the base, so the sewing plate is on the same level as the working table. All these treadles have a tin plated or wooden cover. Many of these covers have been lost over the years. Photograph and information courtesy of Georg Reinfelder. c. between 1918 and 1939.

Quote from Georg: "These three sisters appear to be posing in domestic happiness. Perhaps, their proud father, Friedrich Wilhelm Müller, brought his daughters to be photographed in Berlin, Germany. It must be about 1930."

Plate 460. Her Royal Highness, "No. 1 PRINCESS," is very similar to the Ideal treadle. The sewing machine and the drive wheels are the same, but the cast-iron treadle is different with the following lettering: "No. 1 PRINCESS DECKER MFG. CO. LIMITED DETROIT MICH." This machine has a larger sewing plate than the Ideal treadle. The foot pedal is very ornate. In order to accommodate girls of different heights, the treadle is adjustable in three positions. Photograph and information courtesy of Georg Reinfelder. c. about 1900.

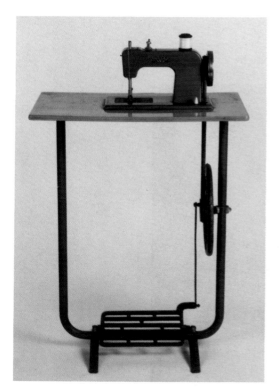

Plate 461. This treadle came from Spain and has a modern steel construction. The foot pedal and the drive wheels are cast iron. Color is light green. The sewing plate is 23" above the floor and is the same level as the wooden working table. "UREK MADE IN SPAIN" is on the machine. The stitch length can be varied. Another model is available without the foot pedal and is hand driven. Photograph and information courtesy of Georg Reinfelder. c. 1955.

Plate 462. STITCHWELL toy treadle is made on an oak stand with two drawers. The machine, fly wheel, and foot pedal are cast iron. National Sewing Machine Company of Belevidere, Illinois is the manufacturer. The head of this machine is almost identical to the hand model Stitchwell. The flywheel is 3½" in diameter and the drive wheel is 7½" in diameter. Montgomery Ward Catalog featured this toy in their Fall and Winter Catalog of 1926-27. Photograph courtesy of Robert Brucato. c. 1920s.

Miscellaneous Miniatures

The tiny sewing machines in this chapter are only a few of the unique and delightful miniatures that are available. Some are the replicas of the real sewing machines built to scale. The funny novelty machines add a humorous touch to the sewing room. Several have been photographed with a thimble to show the small size. This is an ideal collectible for someone with limited display space. Most of the tiny treadles are manufactured specifically for the sewing room of the doll houses. None of these machines actually sew.

Plate 463. Bank, porcelain. 4¾"h x 2"d x 4"w.

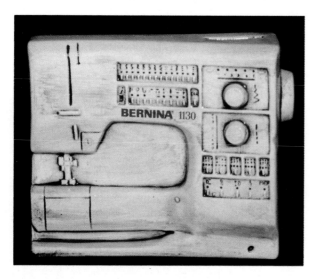

Plate 464 and 465. 1993 was the year Fritz Gegauf, Ltd., the Swiss manufacturer of BERNINA sewing machines and owner of Bernina of America, Inc. celebrated its 100th anniversary. In 1893, Karl Friedrich Gegauf invented the world's first hemstitch sewing machine. By the turn of the century, this machine was not only known in the trade, but was also appreciated by home sewers who actually gave the name "gegaufing" to machine hemstitching. In 1932, the first household sewing machine under the name Bernina was produced. The name symbolizes a majestic Swiss mountain near St. Moritz. A toy sewing machine was manufactured with the name Bernina (not shown.) Promotional items were available at trade shows. The Bernina ceramic bank and button are two of these items. Information furnished by Pat Aulds, Ace Sewing Center, Wichita Falls, Texas. Bank owned by Pat Aulds. Bank: 5¾"h" x 3¼"d x 7"w; button: ¾"h x 1"w.

Plate 466. Christmas ornament by Enesco Corp. "Sew Christmasy," Item #583820. Photograph courtesy of Enesco. 3"h x 4"d x 4"w; c. 1992–1994.

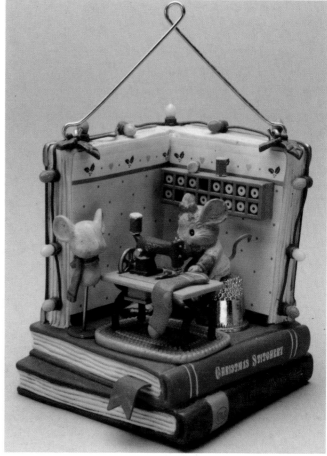

Plate 467. Christmas ornament. 3"h x 1½"d x 2½"w.

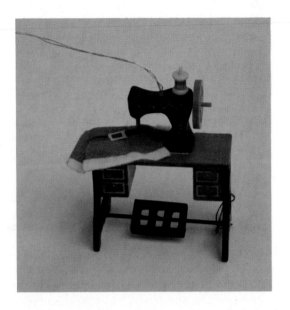

Plate 468. Christmas ornament, "Sewing Santa's Clothes." Made of wood. Photograph courtesy of Claire Toschi. 3⅞"h x 1¾"d x 2¾"w.

Plate 469. Sewing machine watch with tape measure band "Time to Sew."

Plate 470. Sewing machine pin. ¾" h x 1"w.

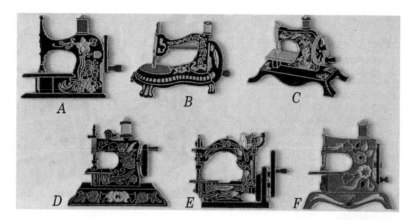

Plate 471. Replicas of sewing machines made into pins from the catalog of Clotilde, Inc., 2 Sew Smart Way B8031, Stevens Point, WI 54481-8031
A. F. W. Müller toy sewing machine.
B. William Jones sewing machine.
C. Red Riding Hood, Casige toy sewing machine.
D. Poppies, Casige sewing machine.
E. Wilcox and Gibbs sewing machine.
F. Lindstrom toy sewing machine.

Plate 472. Silver charms.

Plate 473. Silver charms.

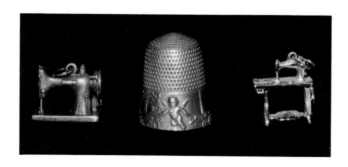

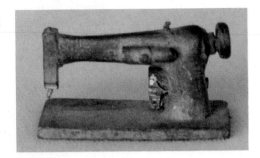

Plate 474. Miniature, pewter. ¾"h x ½"d x 1¼"w.

Plate 475. Miniature, metal. 1⅛"h x ¾"d x 1⅝"w.

Plate 476. Miniature, brass. 1¾"h x 1¼"d x 2¼"w.

Plate 477. Miniature, brass. 1½"h x 1"d x 2¼"w.

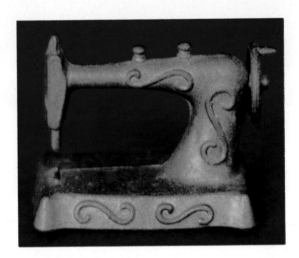

Plate 478. Miniature, pewter. Made in England. 1½"h x 1"d x 2"w.

Plate 479. Miniature, brass. Made in England. 1½"h x 1"d x 2"w.

Plate 480. Miniature, plastic, Galoob. 1¾"h x ¾"d x 2¼"w.

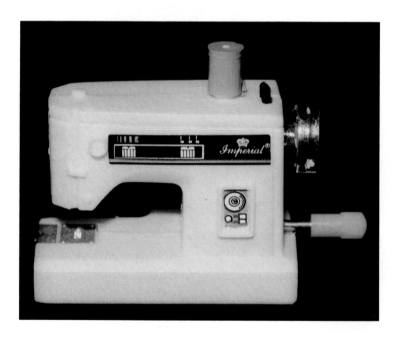

Plate 481. Miniature, plastic, Imperial. 1¾"h x ¾"d x 2½"w.

Plate 482. Miniatures, tiny brass. 1"h x ½"d x 1"w.

Plate 483. Miniatures metal, Singer. Clotilde, Inc. 1⅛"h x ½"d x 1⅜"w.

Plate 484. Miniature, metal. 1"h x ½"d x 1⅜"w.

Plate 485. Miniature, metal. 1½"h x 1½"d x 2½"w.

Plate 486. Miniature, plastic. 1"h x ¼"d x 1"w.

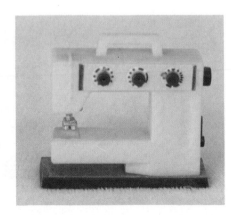

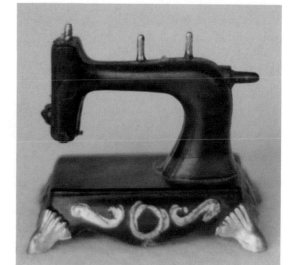

Plate 487. Miniature, plastic. 1½"h x 1"d x 1¾"w.

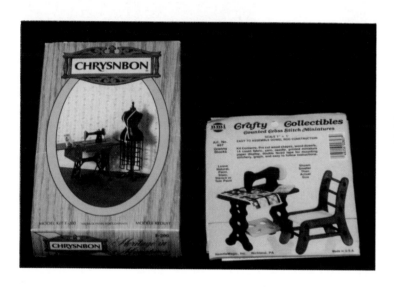

Plate 488. Craft kits. Chrysnbon treadle from Crafty Collectibles.

Plate 489. Craft Kit. Made from plastic and wood. 6"h x 2¾"d x 5"w.

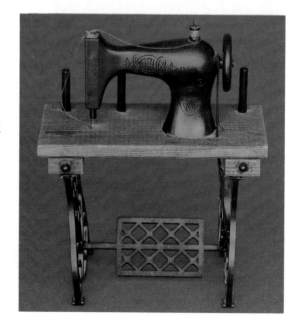

Plate 490. Miniature, tin. Made in Hong Kong. 4¼"h x 3½"d x 5½"w.

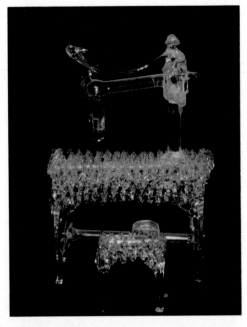

Plate 491. Miniature, blown glass. 5¼"h x 1¾"d x 3½"w.

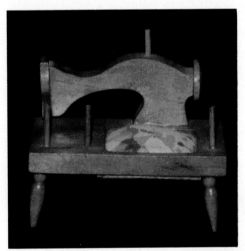

Plate 492. Miniature wood spool holder. 3¾"h x 2¼"d x 4¼"w.

Plate 493. Miniature wood and plastic novelty. 2"h x 1½"d x 5"w.

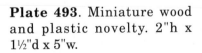

Plate 494. Miniature, wood. Schneider-Garmisch, Germany. 1¾"h x ¾"d x 2½"w.

Plate 495. Pencil sharpeners. Made in Hong Kong. 2"h x 1½"d x 2½"w.

Plate 496. Pin cushion, ceramic bisque. 2¾"h x 1½"d x 3¼"w.

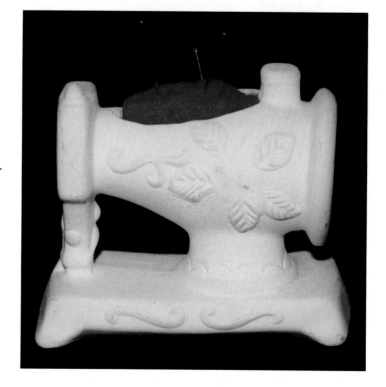

Plate 497. Pin cushion and tape measure. Porcelain. 2¾"h x 2¼"d x 5"w.

Plate 498. Planter, ceramic. 5"h x 3¼"d x 4½"w.

Plate 499. Planter, ceramic. 6"h x 3½"d x 5"w.

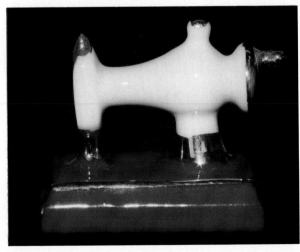

Plate 500. Porcelain miniature. 1½"h x 1"d x 2"w.

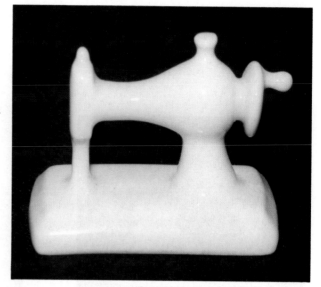

Plate 501. Porcelain miniature. Limoges, made in France. 1½"h x 1"d x 1¾"w.

Plate 502 and 503. Porcelain miniatures. Left: 1¼"h x ¾"d x 1¼"; right: made by Reutter, Denkendorf, Germany. 1"h x ½"d x 1¼"w.

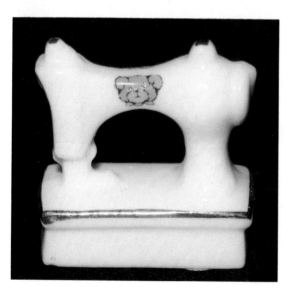

Plate 504. Porcelain miniature, 1985 Enesco. Made in Taiwan. 1½"h x ¾"d x 1½"w.

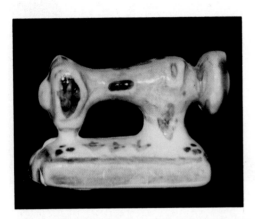

Plate 505. Porcelain miniature. Made in Germany. 1½"h x 1"d x 2¼"w.

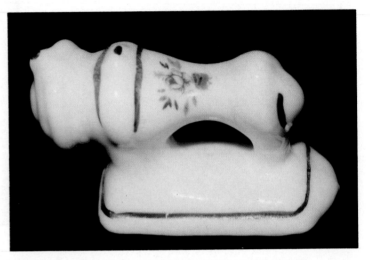

Plate 506. Porcelain miniature. 1½"h x 1"d x 2½"w.

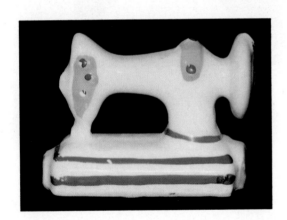

Plate 507. Porcelain miniature. 1½"h x 1"d x 2¼"w.

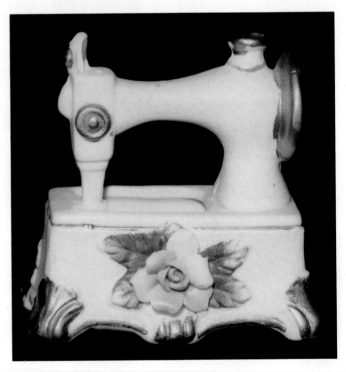

Plate 508. Porcelain miniature. Norleans, made in Taiwan. 2¾"h x 1½"d x 2¾"w.

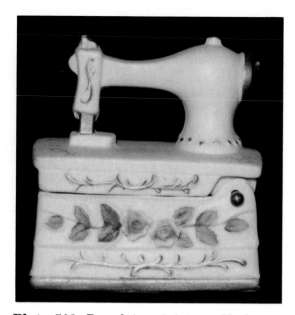

Plate 509. Porcelain miniature. Norleans, Taiwan. Top raises for storage inside. 3½"h x 1¾"d x 3¼"w.

Plate 510. Porcelain miniature. Norleans, made in Taiwan. Top raises for storage inside. 3¼"h x 2"d x 3½"w.

Plate 511. Porcelain miniature, Enesco. 1½"h x1½"d x 1¼"w.

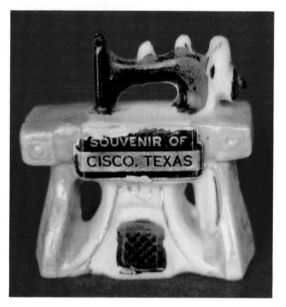

Plate 512. Porcelain, souvenir. Made in Japan. 2¼"h x 1"d x 2¼"w.

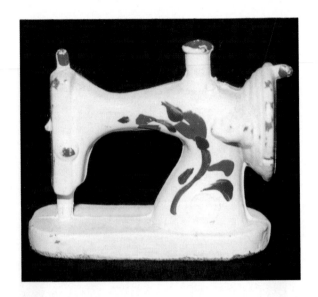

Plate 513. Salt shaker, metal. The pepper shaker (not shown) is black. 1¾"h x ¾"d x 2¼"w.

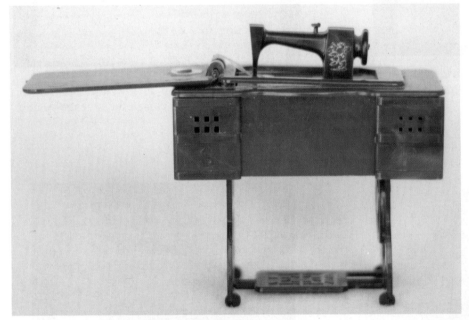

Plate 514. Salt and pepper shaker, plastic. One drawer is pepper, and the other is salt. The head folds down like a real treadle. 3"h x 1¾"d x 3¼"w.

Plate 515. Tins for storage. Square: 4½"h x 5"d x 6"; round: 2¾"d x 7" diameter.

Plate 516. Tin waste basket. 13"h x 6¾"d x 10"w.

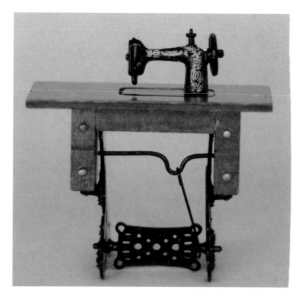

Plate 517. Treadle for doll houses, wood and metal. 3¼"h x 1½"d x 3⅛"w.

Plate 518. Treadle for doll house, metal and wood. Drawers pull out. 3¼"h x 1½"d x 3¼"w.

Plate 519. Treadle for doll house, wood. Made in Taiwan. 2½"h x 1¼"d x 3¼"w.

Plate 521. Treadle for doll house, wood & metal. Henning, made in Germany. Made to scale. Photograph courtesy of Claire Toschi. 3⅛"h x 1¾"d x 3⅛"w.

Plate 520. Treadle for doll house, metal and wood. 3"h x 1½"d x 3⅛"w.

Plate 522. Treadle for doll house, metal. Intricate detail on head. 4"h x 1½"d x 3½"w.

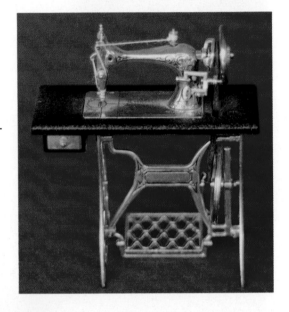

Plate 523. Treadle for doll house, metal. Made in Mexico. 4"h x 2"d x 4"w.

Plate 524. Treadle for doll house, metal. Made in Mexico. 4"h x 2"d x 4"w.

Plate 525. Treadles for doll houses, metal. 1⅛"h x ½"d x 1"w.

Plate 526. Treadle for doll house, metal. 2"h x ¾"w x 1½"w.

Plate 527. Treadle for doll house. Photograph courtesy of Pauline Glidden Toy Museum. 1⅞"h x 1"d x 2⅛"w.

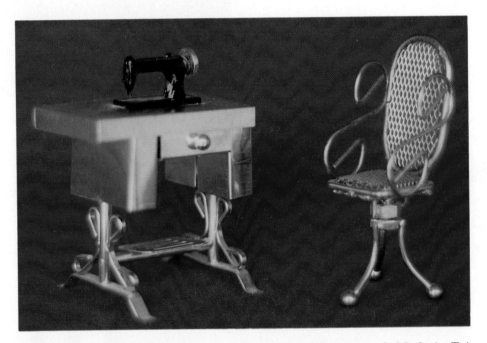

Plate 528. Treadle for doll house with matching chair, metal. Made in Taiwan. 2¼"h x 1½"d x 2½"w.

Plate 529. Treadle for doll house. Turn handle and needle goes up and down. Treadle rocks and two drawers pull out. Lifting a flap at the rear allows the machine to fold. Photograph courtesy of Cumberland Toy and Model Museum. 3¼"w.

Plate 530. Treadle for doll house, metal.
3"h x ¾"d x 1¾"w.

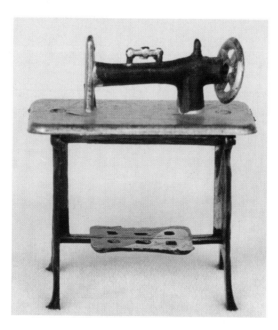

Plate 531. Treadle for doll house, metal.
1¾"h x ¾"d x 1½"w.

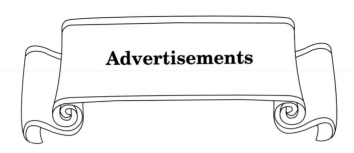

Advertisements

This chapter features pictures and advertisements from old catalogs and magazines. Many of the advertisements have been secured from microfilm. Some of the catalogs were about 100 years old when they were put on microfilm. The pages were very thin and some of the material showed through from the back side. Other advertisements are copies. The quality of the pictures may not be excellent, however the quantity of information is. Old advertisements are an excellent way to date sewing machines.

Perfection Automatic. Sears, Roebuck, & Co. Catalog No. 112, 1903.

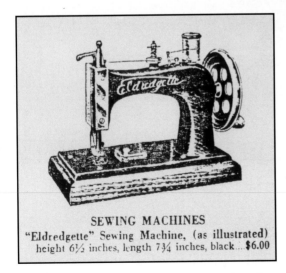

"Eldredgette." F. A. O. Schwarz Catalog, Christmas 1929. Advertisement furnished by Majorie Abel.

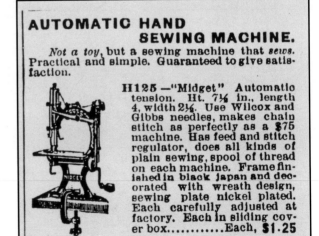

Midget. Butler Brothers Catalog, 1906. Advertisement furnished by Marjorie Abel.

Ladies Home Journal, December 1895. Advertisement furnished by Marjorie Abel.

Sears, Roebuck, & Co. Catalog 1900 and 1902.

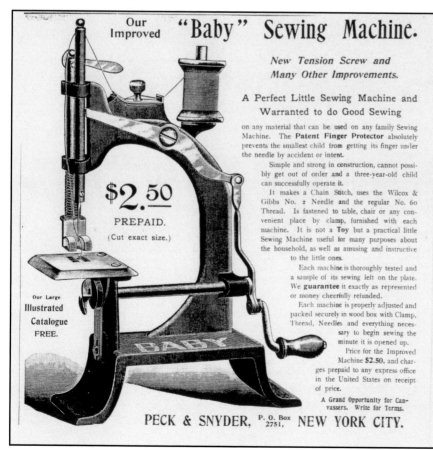

The *Youth's Companion Magazine*, January 3, 1895. Advertisement furnished by Marjorie Abel.

Toy Sewing Machines.

H 10955— "Pony" Sewing Machine, automatic tension, neat in design, elegantly enameled and finished in floral designs of different colors; fastens to a table with a clamp which accompanies each machine; makes Wilcox and Gibbs stitch, and will do plain sewing after operator has learned to run it; has patent feed motion and perfect stitch regulator; uses Wilcox and Gibbs self-setting needle, which has a short blade and long shank not easily broken. A small, light running sewing machine for the little housekeeper on which all kinds of plain sewing may be done. Especially adapted for kindergarten use. Extra clamp and needle sent with each machine. Shipping weight, 2 lb. Each.................................$1.50

Pony. Montgomery Ward Catalog, Fall and Winter, 1904–1905.

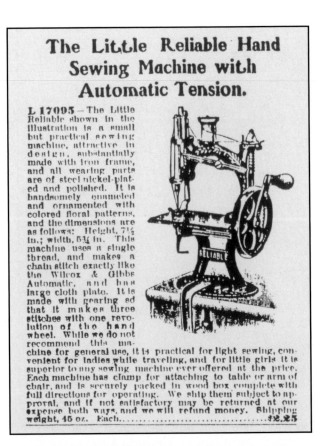

The Little Reliable Hand Sewing Machine with Automatic Tension.

L 17005— The Little Reliable shown in the illustration is a small but practical sewing machine, attractive in design, substantially made with iron frame, and all wearing parts are of steel nickel-plated and polished. It is handsomely enameled and ornamented with colored floral patterns, and the dimensions are as follows: Height, 7½ in.; width, 5¾ in. This machine uses a single thread, and makes a chain stitch exactly like the Wilcox & Gibbs Automatic, and has large cloth plate. It is made with gearing so that it makes three stitches with one revolution of the hand wheel. While we do not recommend this machine for general use, it is practical for light sewing, convenient for ladies while traveling, and for little girls it is superior to any sewing machine ever offered at the price. Each machine has clamp for attaching to table or arm of chair, and is securely packed in wood box complete with full directions for operating. We ship them subject to approval, and if not satisfactory may be returned at our expense both ways, and we will refund money. Shipping weight, 45 oz. Each.................................$2.25

Little Reliable. Montgomery Ward Catalogs, shown from 1905 to 1908.

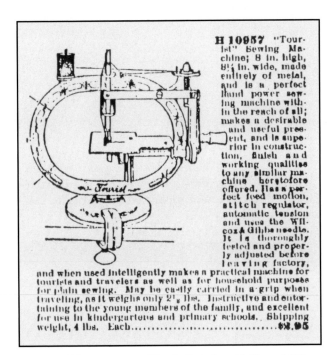

H 10957 "Tourist" Sewing Machine; 8 in. high, 8½ in. wide, made entirely of metal, and is a perfect hand power sewing machine within the reach of all; makes a desirable and useful present, and is superior in construction, finish and working qualities to any similar machine heretofore offered. Has a perfect feed motion, stitch regulator, automatic tension and uses the Wilcox & Gibbs needle. It is thoroughly tested and properly adjusted before leaving factory, and when used intelligently makes a practical machine for tourists and travelers as well as for household purposes for plain sewing. May be easily carried in a grip when traveling, as it weighs only 2½ lbs. Instructive and entertaining to the young members of the family, and excellent for use in kindergartens and primary schools. Shipping weight, 4 lbs. Each.................................$2.95

Tourist. Montgomery Ward Catalog, Fall and Winter, 1903–1904.

Juvenile Chain Stitch Sewing Machine
For Little Women

The Machine illustrated here is a perfect miniature Sewing Machine that within its limitations will sew satisfactorily and well. The dimensions are as follows: Base, 5¾ x 3¼ inches; height of arm, 4½ inches; length of arm, 4¾ inches. It is finished in black enamel with handsome decorations done in three colors. It makes the Elastic Chain Stitch, which may, if it is desired, be instantly unraveled. It uses but one thread; it has No Shuttle. It is adjusted to one size of stitch and to one set degree of tension. It is equipped with two Self-setting needles, one cloth guide, one enameled clamp and screw for fastening machine to table. Packed in substantial wood box with Handy Sliding Cover. Weight, ready for shipment, 6½ pounds.

86B92—Juvenile Sewing Machine, as described above. Each.................................$2.75

Juvenile. Montgomery Ward Catalogs, shown from 1905–1916.

Toy section of Montgomery Ward Catalog 1926-1927.

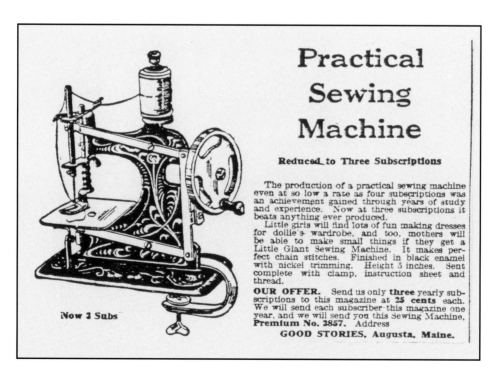

Good Stories Magazine, Augusta, Maine, December 1933. Advertisement furnished by Marjorie Abel.

THINK of having a sewing machine of your very own! One to keep in your own room. Think of the fun you and your friends can have and the practical things you can make with it! Simple garments for yourself, little gifts, towels, aprons, and other plain sewing for mother!

You'll be surprised what you can do with the Singer "20". For it is not a toy, it's a sturdy junior sewing machine for girls, that sews beautifully with a perfect even stitch. It's so easy to set up and use that both you and mother will find it convenient for quick sewing. And it is so small and compact that you can tuck it in the corner of a bag or trunk for use on trips or vacations.

Best of all, it costs so little that every girl can surely have one.

The Singer #20
A JUNIOR MACHINE FOR GIRLS

This is the Singer "20" a practical, portable, junior sewing machine for girls. Easily and quickly fastened to any table edge. Sews perfectly. Strong, well-built, safe—special presser foot protects fingers. Comes in strong box with needles, table clamp and all necessary equipment.

Mothers! There's no better way to interest and encourage your daughter in sewing than to get her a Singer "20". It is practical, instructive, useful and amusing. You can get one, in an attractive gift package, for only $5 at any Singer Shop. ($6 in Canada.) Or, if more convenient, simply use coupon, and we will send you one by mail. (You can pay the postman).

SINGER
SEWING MACHINES

Singer Sewing Machine Co. Inc.,
Dept. 37-L, Singer Bldg., New York

Please send me a little Singer "20" sewing machine, and I will pay the postman when he brings it. (Note—Of course you may send the $5 now if you prefer.)

Name...

Address ....

City.. State....................................

St. Nicholas magazine, November 1926.

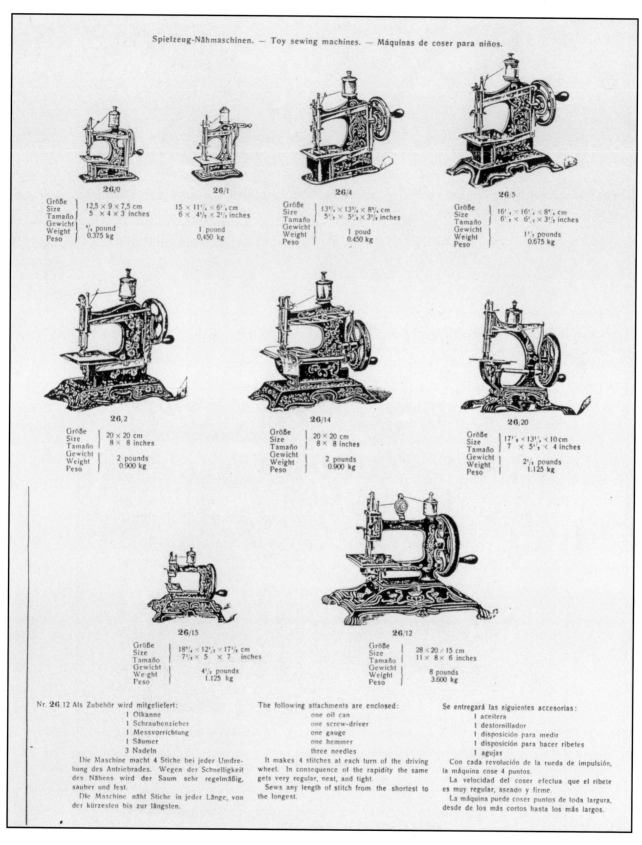

German Toys. Der Universal-Spielwaren-Katalog, 1924–1926. Advertisement furnished by Marjorie Abel.

Stitchwell. Montgomery Ward Catalog, Fall
and Winter 1921–1922.

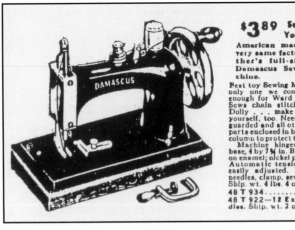

Damascus, Montgomery Ward Christmas Catalog 1940.

Sears, Roebuck, and Co. Catalog 1926.

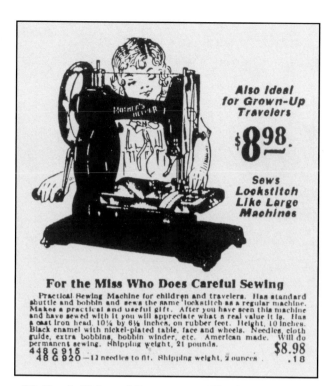

For the Miss Who Does Careful Sewing

Practical Sewing Machine for children and travelers. Has standard shuttle and bobbin and sews the same lockstitch as a regular machine. Makes a practical and useful gift. After you have seen this machine and have sewed with it you will appreciate what a real value it is. Has a cast iron head, 10¼ by 6½ inches, on rubber feet. Height, 10 inches. Black enamel with nickel-plated table, face and wheels. Needles, cloth guide, extra bobbins, bobbin winder, etc. American made. Will do permanent sewing. Shipping weight, 21 pounds.

48 G 915 — $8.98
48 G 920 — 12 needles to fit. Shipping weight, 2 ounces . .18

Mother's Helper. Montgomery Ward Catalog, Fall & Winter, 1927-1928.

Rachel and her "Singer"

A. - A TRUE CLASSIC! Handcrafted metal replica of original 1920 design. Includes iron table clamp and users' manual. Sewing machine (#646) $100.00.

Singer Reproduction. Anne Powell, Ltd. Catalog, 1990.

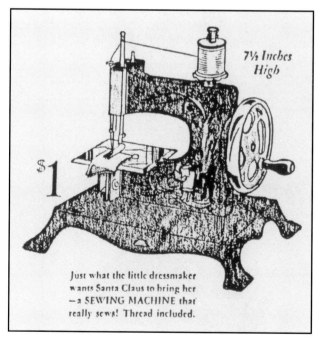

Just what the little dressmaker wants Santa Claus to bring her —a SEWING MACHINE that really sews! Thread included.

Casige with Red Riding Hood & the Wolf. Kresge's 25¢ to $1.00. Catalog 1938. Advertisement furnished by Marjorie Abel.

Oklahoma Tire & Supply Co. "Otasco." Catalog of 1957. Advertisement furnished by Marjorie Abel.

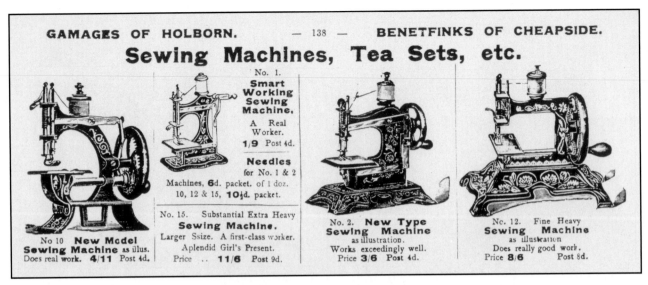

Gamages Christmas Bazaar, 1913.

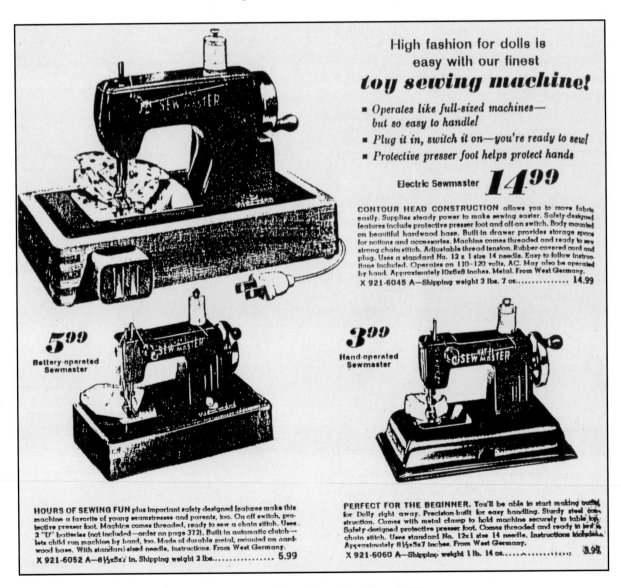

J. C. Penney Christmas Catalog, 1965.

Life Magazine, September 1954.

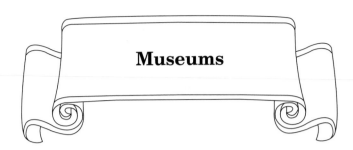

Museums

Many letters were sent to museums seeking information regarding their collection of sewing machines, toy sewing machines, and textiles. Listed below are the museums that replied to the inquiry. Several of the museums only have a few toy sewing machines, but the toy enthusiast and the young at heart will enjoy visiting them. Since the hours and seasons vary, it would be wise to call for opening times.

Canada

Surrey Museum
6022–176th Street, Cloverdale
Surrey, British Columbia
Canada V3S 4E8
Phone 604-574-5744

This museum has 42 sewing machines on display (4 are toys). Two displays specifically focus on sewing machines. The museum consists of three historic sites: Museum Archives, Surrey Museum, and Historic Stewart Farmhouse.

Ukrainian Museum of Canada
620 Spadina Ave.
Toronto, Ontario
Phone: 416-923-3318

This museum does not have sewing machines, but specializes in Ukrainian embroideries, textiles, and ceramics. Hours: Tuesday to Friday 1–4 pm, all year round.

France

Collection THIMONNIER-DOYEN
11 rue de la Paix
69660 SAINT GERMAIN AU MONT D' OR FRANCE
Call 78.35.86.24 for appointment.

This collection consists of many old and rare sewing machines and specializes in machines before 1900.

Germany

Toy collection of Ivan Steiger
Spielzeugmuseum
Marienplatz, München
Phone: 089-29-4001
Hours: Mon-Sat 10am to 5:30 pm.
Sun & Holidays 10am to 6pm.

Das Spielzeugmuseum
Residenzplatz, Passau
Hours: daily 9 am to 6 pm;
winter hours posted

See photograph in this book of F. W. Müller toy sewing machine. Many dolls and other toys are featured at the museum.

Historical Sewing Machine and Iron Museum
Historisches Nähmaschinen & Bugelusen Museum
Heimeranstrasse, 68-70
München
Phone: 089-510880
Hours: Mon-Fri 10am to 4pm,
closed Sat, Sun, and holidays

The display has 150 sewing machines. A special silver machine of the Family Kayser is on display. No toy sewing machines are displayed at this time.

Great Britain

Bethnal Green Museum of Childhood
Cambridge Heath Road
London E 29PA England
Recorded information 081-980-2415

This museum contains toy machines of American, British, and German origin ranging from 1900-1970. The collection includes a toy treadle and a few miniature sewing machines.

The Chester Toy and Doll Museum
13A Lower Bridge Street Row
Chester CHI IRS England
Phone: 0244,346297
Open 7 days 11 am to 5 pm.

Over 7000 toys are on display (one toy sewing machine), and a toy shop has a varied collection of antique and collectible items.

Cumberland Toy and Model Museum
Banks Court, Market Place
Cockermouth, Cumbria, England
Hours: Open every day from Feb. 1st to Nov. 30th
Dec. – Jan. by appointment (0900) 827606.

Their vast toy collection contains several toy sewing machines. Photographs of these are displayed throughout this book.

Dewsbury Museum
Crow Nest Park
Heckmondivike Road
Dewsbury, England
Phone 0924,468171

The "Magic Theme of Childhood" is the theme for this museum.

Luton Museum Service
Wardown Park
Luton LU2 7HA, England
Phone: (0582) 36941 or 36942

The majority of items in this collection relate to the local hat industry, but there are some toy and miniature sewing machines. The most interesting is a cast iron in the form of a clown. It bears the trademark of an arm holding a balance. Others are chain stitch machines. The toy sewing machines can be seen by appointment.

Museum of Childhood
42 High Street
Edinburgh EH1 1TG, Scotland
Phone: 0312, 252424

This museum has toy sewing machines on display. There are five public galleries. A list of the contents sounds like a magical department store filled with memories of the joys and tribulations of childhood.

Museum of Childhood

Museum of English Rural Lift
University of Reading
Whiteknights, Reading RG62AG, England
Phone: 0734 318660

This museum has many (over 100) sewing machines, including toy sewing machines from the collection of J.N. Barnett. He bequeathed his collection of sewing machines to the university. See a booklet "Sewing Machines—A Catalog of the Barnett Collection" ISBN # 0-7049-0494 2.

Museum of Childhood
1 Castle Street, Beaumaris
Isle of Anglesey
Gwymnedd, LL58 8AP, Wales
Phone: (0248) 712498

This museum's collection of over 2000 items is housed in nine rooms, each room having a different theme in family life. The collection includes several toy sewing machines and miniatures for doll houses.

Pollock's Toy Museum
1 Scala Street
London W. 1, England
Phone: 0716 363452
Hours 10am to 5pm, Monday– Saturday, closed Sundays and holidays.

Toy enthusiasts will enjoy the intriguing displays of dolls and toys. Five toy sewing machines are on display, including one from Portugal.

Science Museum
Exhibition Road, South Kensington
London SW7 Phone: 071-938-5336

Many sewing machines are owned by this museum, however, they do not have many on view. Call in advance for arrangements to see the collection at Blyth House in Kensington.

Tolson Memorial Museum
Ravensknowle Park
Huddersfield HD 5 80, England
Phone 0484-530591

Although this museum only has two toy sewing machines, you will find many displays of textile history.

Switzerland

Sewing Machine Museum
Bernina Sewing Machine Works
CH-8266 Steckborn, Switzerland

The museum is located at the factory and can be visited by anyone on application. The history of the sewing machine can be followed. Machines can be seen from a large number of countries illustrating the progress from the earliest times to the mass production era.

USA

California
Singer Dealer Museum
3400 Park Boulevard
Oakland, California 94610
Phone: (510) 261-0413

This is a private collection of antique American sewing machines (no toys) dating from 1853–1900 and over a thousand pieces of related advertising material. By appointment only.

Colorado

Denver Museum of Miniatures, Dolls, and Toys
1880 Gaylord Street
Denver, Colorado 80206
Recording: (303) 322-3704

Visitors to the museum can be magically transformed to an earlier era...learning about architecture, interior design, lifestyles, fashion, furniture, art, and more importantly...the folklore of an earlier time. At the present, only two toy sewing machines are in their collection.

Michigan

Henry Ford Museum and Greenfield Village
Dearborn, Michigan
Phone: (313) 271-1620
This museum has several examples of small machines, but none are toys.

Missouri

Toy and Miniature Museum
5235 Oak Street
Kansas City, Missouri 64112
Phone: (816) 333 2055

The fabulous toy exhibits will delight all the young at heart. Three toy sewing machines are on display.

Eugene Field House & Toy Museum
634 South Broadway
St. Louis, Missouri 63102
Phone: (314) 421-4689

This is the childhood home of the "Children's Poet." They have a group of miniature rooms by Ann K. Pipe, one of which is a complete sewing room that does contain a miniature sewing machine.

Nebraska

Harold Warp Pioneer Village Foundation
P. O. Box 68, 12 Miles South of I-80 at exit 279
Minden, Nebraska 68959
Phone 1-800-445-4447
Hours: 8:00am to sundown, 7 days a week.

This is a museum of progress, with over 50,000 items in 28 buildings on 20 acres, with motel and campground. Their collection does include many toy sewing machines and domestic sewing machines. See the "Mother's Helper" by New Home photograph in this book.

New Hampshire

Whipple House Museum & Pauline Glidden Toy Museum
Pleasant Street, P. O. Box 17
Ashland, New Hampshire 03217
Hours: Wed–Sat.1:00–4:00 pm; July– Labor Day.
Open for group hours by appointment.

The toy museum has more than one thousand antique children's toys acquired by Pauline Glidden and visitors have been pleasantly surprised by the quality and extent of the collection. Two toy sewing machines are on display.

New York

Strong Museum
One Manhattan Square
Rochester, New York 14607
Phone (716) 263-2700

This museum's collection includes 61 toy sewing machines and 31 adult sewing machines.

South Dakota

Enchanted World Doll Museum
615 North Main
Mitchell, South Dakota 57301
Phone: (605) 996-9896

Many toys sewing machines are used as accessories with the dolls in the dioramas. More than 4000 dolls are on display in nearly 400 scenes. A few scenes with toy sewing machines are: "Sewing School," "Sewing Bee," and "At the Dressmaker's." This museum is internationally recognized as one of the best doll museums in the world.

Enchanted World Doll Museum

Enchanted World Doll Museum

241

Texas

Antique Sewing Machine Museum
804 Abram
Arlington, Texas 76013
Phone (817) 275-0971
Hours: Tue–Sat 9am–5pm.
Sunday–1pm–5pm

This private museum has over 90 antique machines, a few toy sewing machines, antique buttons, patterns, and other memorabilia. Frank Smith Owner.

Bauer Toy Museum
233 E. Main
Fredericksburg, Texas 78624
Phone: (210) 997-9394
hours: Wed–Mon. 10am – 5pm.

Over 2000 toys from 1870 to the Star Wars era are on display including several toy sewing machines.

Vermont

Shelburne Museum
US Rte. 7, P. O. Box 10
Shelburne,Vermont 05482
Taped information: (802) 985-3346

This museum has an extensive toy collection, including a tiny miniature sewing machine in a doll house. Explore 37 exhibit buildings and stroll through 45 scenic areas.

Antique Sewing Machine Museum

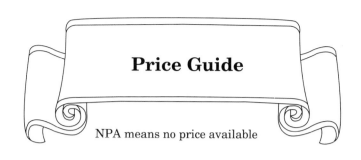

Price Guide

NPA means no price available

Plate 1. Artcraft	$65.00 – $85.00
Plate 2. Artcraft	$65.00 – $85.00
Plate 3. Artcraft	$65.00 – $85.00
Plate 4. Artcraft	$75.00 – $95.00
Plate 5. Artcraft	$50.00 – $75.00
Plate 6. Artcraft	$50.00 – $75.00
Plate 7. Baby	$200.00 – $250.00
Plate 8. Batchelor & Stenson	NPA
Plate 9. Betsy Ross	$75.00 – $100.00
Plate 10. Betsy Ross	$75.00 – $100.00
Plate 11. Betsy Ross	$75.00 – $95.00
Plate 12. Betsy Ross	$75.00 – $95.00
Plate 13. Bing	NPA
Plate 14. Bing	NPA
Plate 15. Bloomingdales	NPA
Plate 16. Bremer & Brückmann	NPA
Plate 17. Britains Petite	$30.00 – $40.00
Plate 18. Britains Petite	$15.00 – $25.00
Plate 19. Britains Petite	$15.00 – $25.00
Plate 20. Brother	$75.00 – $100.00
Plate 21. Brother	$75.00 – $100.00
Plate 22. Casige	NPA
Plate 23. Casige	NPA
Plate 24. Casige	NPA
Plate 25. Casige	$100.00 – $135.00
Plate 26. Casige	$100.00 – $135.00
Plate 27. Casige	$100.00 – $135.00
Plate 28. Casige	$100.00 – $135.00
Plate 29. Casige	$100.00 – $135.00
Plate 30. Casige	$75.00 – $95.00
Plate 31. Casige	$75.00 – $95.00
Plate 32. Casige	$75.00 – $95.00
Plate 33. Casige	$75.00 – $95.00
Plate 34. Casige	$75.00 – $95.00
Plate 35. Casige	$85.00 – $100.00
Plate 36. Casige	$85.00 – $100.00
Plate 37. Casige	$125.00 – $175.00
Plate 38. Casige	$125.00 – $175.00
Plate 39. Casige	$125.00 – $175.00
Plate 40. Casige	$125.00 – $175.00
Plate 41. Casige	$125.00 – $175.00
Plate 42. Casige	$125.00 – $175.00
Plate 43. Casige	$75.00 – $95.00
Plate 44. Casige	$75.00 – $95.00
Plate 45. Casige	$75.00 – $100.00
Plate 46. Casige	$75.00 – $100.00
Plate 47. Casige	$75.00 – $100.00
Plate 48. Casige	$100.00 – $150.00
Plate 49. Casige	$75.00 – $100.00
Plate 50. Casige	$75.00 – $100.00
Plate 51. Casige	$75.00 – $100.00
Plate 52. Casige	$75.00 – $100.00
Plate 53. Casige	$75.00 – $100.00
Plate 54. Casige	$75.00 – $100.00
Plate 55. Casige	$75.00 – $100.00
Plate 56. Casige	$75.00 – $100.00
Plate 57. Casige	$100.00 – $135.00
Plate 58. Casige	$75.00 – $100.00
Plate 59. Casige	$55.00 – $75.00
Plate 60. Casige	$55.00 – $75.00
Plate 61. Casige	$55.00 – $75.00
Plate 62. Casige	$55.00 – $75.00
Plate 63. Casige	$55.00 – $75.00
Plate 64. Casige	$55.00 – $75.00
Plate 65. Casige	$55.00 – $75.00
Plate 66. Casige	$55.00 – $75.00
Plate 67. Casige	$85.00 – $110.00
Plate 68. Casige	$50.00 – $75.00
Plate 69. Casige	$45.00 – $65.00
Plate 70. China	$15.00 – $35.00
Plate 71. China	NPA
Plate 72. China	$15.00 – $25.00
Plate 73. China	$15.00 – $25.00
Plate 74. China	$10.00 – $20.00
Plate 75. China	$10.00 – $20.00
Plate 76. China	$10.00
Plate 77. China	$12.00
Plate 78. China	$20.00
Plate 79. China	$20.00
Plate 80. China	$15.00 – $25.00
Plate 81. China	$15.00 – $25.00
Plate 82. China	$15.00 – $25.00
Plate 83. China	$50.00
Plate 84. China	$8.00 – $10.00
Plate 85. China	$12.00
Plate 86. China	$10.00
Plate 87. China	$10.00
Plate 88. China	$10.00
Plate 89. China	$8.00
Plate 90. China	$10.00
Plate 91. China	$10.00
Plate 92. China	$15.00

Plate 93. Crystal ....$20.00 – $30.00
Plate 94. Crystal ....$20.00 – $30.00
Plate 95. Crystal ....$20.00 – $30.00
Plate 96. Crystal ....$20.00 – $30.00
Plate 97. Crystal ....$20.00 – $30.00
Plate 98. Crystal ....$20.00 – $30.00
Plate 99. Crystal ....$20.00 – $30.00
Plate 100. Crystal ....$20.00 – $30.00
Plate 101. Crystal ....$25.00 – $45.00
Plate 102. Delta ....$75.00 – $125.00
Plate 103. Dolly Dressmaker............................NPA
Plate 104. Durham ....$15.00 – $25.00
Plate 105. Durham ....$15.00 – $25.00
Plate 106. Durham ....$15.00 – $25.00
Plate 107. Durham ....$15.00 – $25.00
Plate 108. Durham ....$35.00 – $45.00
Plate 109. Durham ....$25.00 – $35.00
Plate 110. Durham ....$25.00 – $35.00
Plate 111. Durham ....$30.00 – $35.00
Plate 112. Durham ....$30.00 – $35.00
Plate 113. Durham ....$20.00 – $35.00
Plate 114. Durham ....$20.00 – $35.00
Plate 115. Durham ....$20.00 – $35.00
Plate 116. Durham ....$20.00 – $30.00
Plate 117. Durham ....$20.00 – $30.00
Plate 118. Durham ....$25.00 – $35.00
Plate 119. Elna................................$100.00 – $150.00
Plate 120. Elna ....$100.00 – $150.00
Plate 121. Elna ....$30.00 – $45.00
Plate 122. England ....$75.00 – $100.00
Plate 123. England ....$75.00 – $100.00
Plate 124. England ....$75.00 – $100.00
Plate 125. England................................NPA
Plate 126. England................................NPA
Plate 127. England................................NPA
Plate 128. England................................NPA
Plate 129. Englewood................................NPA
Plate 130. Essex...............................$100.00 – $130.00
Plate 131. Foley & Williams.........$200.00 – $300.00
Plate 132. Foley & Williams.........$200.00 – $300.00
Plate 133. Foley & Williams.........$200.00 – $300.00
Plate 134. Foley & Williams.........$200.00 – $300.00
Plate 135. Foley & Williams.........$200.00 – $300.00
Plate 136. Foot ....NPA
Plate 137. France ....NPA
Plate 138. France $120.00
Plate 139. France ....NPA
Plate 140. France ....NPA
Plate 141. France ....NPA
Plate 142. France ....NPA
Plate 143. France ....NPA
Plate 144. France ....$25.00 – $50.00
Plate 145. France ....$25.00 – $50.00
Plate 146. Gateway..........................$35.00 – $50.00
Plate 147. Gateway..........................$35.00 – $50.00
Plate 148. Gateway ....$35.00 – $50.00

Plate 149. Gateway..........................$35.00 – $50.00
Plate 150. Gateway..........................$35.00 – $50.00
Plate 151. Gateway..........................$50.00 – $75.00
Plate 152. Gateway..........................$50.00 – $75.00
Plate 153. Gem................................NPA
Plate 154. Genero ....$65.00 – $85.00
Plate 155. Genero ....$50.00 – $75.00
Plate 156. Genero ....$50.00 – $75.00
Plate 157. Genero ....$50.00 – $75.00
Plate 158. Germany ....NPA
Plate 159. Germany ....NPA
Plate 160. Germany ....NPA
Plate 161. Germany ....NPA
Plate 162. Germany ....NPA
Plate 163. Germany ....NPA
Plate 164. Germany ....NPA
Plate 165. Hasbro ....$25.00 – $40.00
Plate 166. Hasbro ....$15.00 – $30.00
Plate 167. Hasbro ....$45.00 – $55.00
Plate 168. Hasbro ....$45.00 – $55.00
Plate 169. Hasbro ....$45.00 – $55.00
Plate 170. Hasbro ....$15.00 – $20.00
Plate 171. Hasbro $20.00
Plate 172. Hoge ....$65.00 – $85.00
Plate 173. Hoge ....$45.00 – $65.00
Plate 174. Hoge ....$45.00 – $65.00
Plate 175. Hoge ....$35.00 – $55.00
Plate 176. Hong Kong...................$35.00 – $55.00
Plate 177. Hong Kong...................$25.00 – $50.00
Plate 178. Hong Kong...................$15.00 – $30.00
Plate 179. Hong Kong...................$15.00 – $30.00
Plate 180. Hong Kong...................$15.00 – $30.00
Plate 181. Hong Kong...................$15.00 – $30.00
Plate 182. Hong Kong...................$15.00 – $30.00
Plate 183. Hong Kong...................$15.00 – $35.00
Plate 184. Husqvarna........................$50.00
Plate 185. Ideal ....NPA
Plate 186. Italy $50.00
Plate 187. Japan $170.00
Plate 188. Japan ....NPA
Plate 189. Japan ....NPA
Plate 190. Japan ....$150.00 – $175.00
Plate 191. Japan ....$150.00 – $175.00
Plate 192. Japan ....$150.00 – $175.00
Plate 193. Japan ....$45.00 – $65.00
Plate 194. Japan ....NPA
Plate 195. Japan ....$40.00 – $60.00
Plate 196. Japan ....$40.00 – $60.00
Plate 197. Japan ....$40.00 – $60.00
Plate 198. Japan ....$40.00 – $60.00
Plate 199. Japan $25.00
Plate 200. Japan $50.00
Plate 201. Japan ....$20.00 – $35.00
Plate 202. Japan ....$20.00 – $35.00
Plate 203. Japan ....$20.00 – $35.00
Plate 204. Japan ....$30.00 – $50.00

Plate 205. Japan.............................$30.00 – $50.00
Plate 206. Japan.............................$30.00 – $50.00
Plate 207. Jaymar..........................$30.00 – $50.00
Plate 208. Jaymar..........................$30.00 – $50.00
Plate 209. Jaymar..........................$30.00 – $50.00
Plate 210. Jaymar..........................$30.00 – $50.00
Plate 211. KAYanEE.....................$50.00 – $75.00
Plate 212. KAYanEE.....................$50.00 – $75.00
Plate 213. KAYanEE.....................$50.00 – $75.00
Plate 214. KAYanEE...................$75.00 – $100.00
Plate 215. KAYanEE...................$75.00 – $100.00
Plate 216. KAYanEE...................$75.00 – $100.00
Plate 217. KAYanEE.................$75.00 – $100.00
Plate 218. KAYanEE.....................$45.00 – $65.00
Plate 219. KAYanEE.....................$45.00 – $65.00
Plate 220. KAYanEE.....................$45.00 – $65.00
Plate 221. KAYanEE.....................$60.00 – $80.00
Plate 222. KAYanEE.....................$60.00 – $80.00
Plate 223. KAYanEE.....................$60.00 – $80.00
Plate 224. KAYanEE.....................$60.00 – $80.00
Plate 225. KAYanEE.....................$60.00 – $80.00
Plate 226. KAYanEE.....................$60.00 – $80.00
Plate 227. KAYanEE.....................$60.00 – $80.00
Plate 228. KAYanEE.....................$35.00 – $50.00
Plate 229. KAYanEE.....................$35.00 – $50.00
Plate 230. KAYanEE.....................$35.00 – $50.00
Plate 231. KAYanEE.....................$35.00 – $50.00
Plate 232. KAYanEE.....................$35.00 – $50.00
Plate 233. KAYanEE.....................$35.00 – $50.00
Plate 234. KAYanEE.....................$35.00 – $50.00
Plate 235. KAYanEE.....................$35.00 – $50.00
Plate 236. KAYanEE.....................$35.00 – $50.00
Plate 237. KAYanEE.....................$35.00 – $50.00
Plate 238. KAYanEE.....................$35.00 – $50.00
Plate 239. KAYanEE.....................$35.00 – $50.00
Plate 240. KAYanEE.....................$35.00 – $50.00
Plate 241. KAYanEE.....................$35.00 – $50.00
Plate 242. KAYanEE.....................$35.00 – $50.00
Plate 243. KAYanEE.....................$35.00 – $50.00
Plate 244. KAYanEE.....................$35.00 – $50.00
Plate 245. KAYanEE.....................$35.00 – $50.00
Plate 246. KAYanEE.....................$35.00 – $50.00
Plate 247. KAYanEE.....................$35.00 – $50.00
Plate 248. KAYanEE.....................$35.00 – $50.00
Plate 249. KAYanEE.....................$35.00 – $50.00
Plate 250. KAYanEE.....................$45.00 – $65.00
Plate 251. KAYanEE.....................$35.00 – $50.00
Plate 252. KAYanEE.....................$35.00 – $50.00
Plate 253. KAYanEE.....................$35.00 – $50.00
Plate 254. Kochs-Adler ....NPA
Plate 255. Lakner...NPA
Plate 256. Lanard............................$6.00 – $12.00
Plate 257. Lanard..................................... $11.00
Plate 258. Lanard.........................$15.00 – $20.00
Plate 259. Liliputian.......................................NPA
Plate 260. Lindstrom....................$75.00 – $100.00
Plate 261. Lindstrom....................$75.00 – $100.00

Plate 262. Lindstrom....................$100.00 – $125.00
Plate 263. Lindstrom....................$100.00 – $125.00
Plate 264. Lindstrom....................$100.00 – $125.00
Plate 265. Lindstrom......................$75.00 – $100.00
Plate 266. Lindstrom......................$75.00 – $100.00
Plate 267. Little Mary ....$50.00 – $75.00
Plate 268. Little Mary ....$50.00 – $75.00
Plate 269. Little Mary ....$50.00 – $75.00
Plate 270. LJN ....$40.00 – $50.00
Plate 271. LJN ....$40.00 – $50.00
Plate 272. Marx ....$50.00 – $75.00
Plate 273. Mattel ....$45.00 – $55.00
Plate 274. Mattel ....$15.00 – $25.00
Plate 275. Mattel ....$20.00 – $30.00
Plate 276. Mattel ....$5.00 – $10.00
Plate 277. Mattel $2.00
Plate 278. Metallograph...............$125.00 – $150.00
Plate 279. Montgomery Ward ....$30.00 – $50.00
Plate 280. Montgomery Ward ....$20.00 – $35.00
Plate 281. Montgomery Ward ....$30.00 – $50.00
Plate 282. Montgomery Ward ....$30.00 – $45.00
Plate 283. Montgomery Ward ....$30.00 – $45.00
Plate 284. Montgomery Ward ....$45.00 – $50.00
Plate 285. Montgomery Ward ....$75.00 – $100.00
Plate 286. Montgomery Ward ....$30.00 – $50.00
Plate 287. Montgomery Ward ....$20.00 – $35.00
Plate 288. Montgomery Ward ....$75.00 – $100.00
Plate 289. Morse ....$75.00 – $100.00
Plate 290. Müller ....$100.00 – $150.00
Plate 291. Müller ....$100.00 – $150.00
Plate 292. Müller (set)................................. $450.00
Plate 293. Müller ....$175.00 – $200.00
Plate 294. Müller ....$100.00 – $150.00
Plate 295. Müller ....$75.00 – $100.00
Plate 296. Müller ....NPA
Plate 297. Müller ....$100.00 – $150.00
Plate 298. Müller ....$100.00 – $135.00
Plate 299. Müller ....$100.00 – $135.00
Plate 300. Müller ....$100.00 – $135.00
Plate 301. Müller ....$125.00 – $150.00
Plate 302. Müller ....$100.00 – $135.00
Plate 303. Müller ....$175.00 – $225.00
Plate 304. Müller ....$175.00 – $225.00
Plate 305. Müller ....$100.00 – $135.00
Plate 306. Müller ....$175.00 – $225.00
Plate 307. Müller ....$175.00 – $225.00
Plate 308. Müller ....$175.00 – $225.00
Plate 309. Müller ....$150.00 – $175.00
Plate 310. Müller ....NPA
Plate 311. Müller ....$90.00 – $100.00
Plate 312. National................................. $150.00
Plate 313. National.................................$150.00
Plate 314. National.................................$150.00
Plate 315. National.................................$150.00
Plate 316. National.................................$150.00
Plate 317. National.................................$100.00
Plate 318. National.................................$100.00

Plate 319. National.................................$100.00	Plate 376. Singer ....$35.00 – $50.00
Plate 320. Necchi ....$65.00 – $85.00	Plate 377. Singer ....$30.00 – $60.00
Plate 321. Necchi ....NPA	Plate 378. Singer ....$30.00 – $50.00
Plate 322. Necchi ....$25.00 – $35.00	Plate 379. Singer ....$30.00 – $50.00
Plate 323. New Home ....NPA	Plate 380. Singer ....$25.00 – $45.00
Plate 324. New Home $150.00	Plate 381. Singer ....$30.00 – $50.00
Plate 325. New Home $150.00	Plate 382. Singer ....$15.00 – $25.00
Plate 326. New Home $10.00	Plate 383. Singer ....$15.00 – $25.00
Plate 327. Penney ....$30.00 – $50.00	Plate 384. Singer $20.00
Plate 328. Penney ....$35.00 – $45.00	Plate 385. Singer $20.00
Plate 329. Penney ....$25.00 – $35.00	Plate 386. Singer $20.00
Plate 330. Pfaff ....$100.00 – $150.00	Plate 387. Singer $50.00
Plate 331. Plank ....NPA	Plate 388. Singer ....$35.00 – $50.00
Plate 332. Pony ....NPA	Plate 389. Singer ....$250.00 – $500.00
Plate 333. Schürhoff ....NPA	Plate 390. Smith & Egge..............$200.00 – $300.00
Plate 334. Sears $100.00	Plate 391. Smith & Egge..............$200.00 – $300.00
Plate 335. Sears ....$30.00 – $50.00	Plate 392. Smith & Egge..............$200.00 – $300.00
Plate 336. Sears ....$30.00 – $50.00	Plate 393. Smith & Egge..............$200.00 – $300.00
Plate 337. Sears ....$30.00 – $50.00	Plate 394. Smith & Egge..............$200.00 – $300.00
Plate 338. Sears ....$30.00 – $50.00	Plate 395. Smith & Egge..............$200.00 – $300.00
Plate 339. Sew-Ette ....$35.00 – $50.00	Plate 396. Smith & Egge..............$200.00 – $300.00
Plate 340. Sew-Ette ....$35.00 – $50.00	Plate 397. Sotoy ....$150.00 – $175.00
Plate 341. Sew-Ette ....$35.00 – $50.00	Plate 398. Sotoy ....NPA
Plate 342. Sew-Ette ....$35.00 – $50.00	Plate 399. Spenser ....NPA
Plate 343. Sew-Ette ....$35.00 – $50.00	Plate 400. Spenser ....NPA
Plate 344. Sew-Ette ....$35.00 – $50.00	Plate 401. Steinfeldt & Blasberg.....................NPA
Plate 345. Sew-Ette ....$35.00 – $50.00	Plate 402. Steinfeldt & Blasberg.....................NPA
Plate 346. Sew-EZ ....$45.00 – $55.00	Plate 403. Straco............................$25.00 – $50.00
Plate 347. Sew-EZ ....$45.00 – $55.00	Plate 404. Straco............................$25.00 – $50.00
Plate 348. Sew-Mate.........................$35.00 – $50.00	Plate 405. Straco............................$25.00 – $50.00
Plate 349. Sew-Mate.........................$35.00 – $50.00	Plate 406. Straco............................$25.00 – $50.00
Plate 350. Sew-Mate.........................$35.00 – $50.00	Plate 407. Straco............................$25.00 – $50.00
Plate 351. Sew-Mate.........................$35.00 – $50.00	Plate 408. Straco............................$25.00 – $50.00
Plate 352. Sew-Mate.........................$35.00 – $50.00	Plate 409. Straco............................$25.00 – $50.00
Plate 353. Sew-Mate.........................$30.00 – $40.00	Plate 410. Straco............................$35.00 – $55.00
Plate 354. Singer ....$175.00 – $225.00	Plate 411. Straco............................$35.00 – $55.00
Plate 355. Singer ....$150.00 – $175.00	Plate 412. Straco............................$35.00 – $55.00
Plate 356. Singer ....$125.00 – $150.00	Plate 413. Straco............................$25.00 – $50.00
Plate 357. Singer ....$125.00 – $150.00	Plate 414. Straco............................$35.00 – $55.00
Plate 358. Singer...................................NPA	Plate 415. Straco............................$35.00 – $55.00
Plate 359. Singer ....$125.00 – $150.00	Plate 416. Straco............................$25.00 – $50.00
Plate 360. Singer $135.00	Plate 417. Straco............................$25.00 – $50.00
Plate 361. Singer...................................NPA	Plate 418. Straco ....NPA
Plate 362. Singer ....$175.00 – $250.00	Plate 419. Tabitha..................................NPA
Plate 363. Singer ....$100.00 – $125.00	Plate 420. Taiwan...................................$25.00
Plate 364. Singer...................................NPA	Plate 421. Tomy.....................................NPA
Plate 365. Singer ....$150.00 – $175.00	Plate 422. Tomy.....................................NPA
Plate 366. Singer...................................NPA	Plate 423. Tourist..................................NPA
Plate 367. Singer...................................NPA	Plate 424. Triumph..................................NPA
Plate 368. Singer ....$100.00 – $125.00	Plate 425. USA ....NPA
Plate 369. Singer ....$100.00 – $125.00	Plate 426. USA ....$10.00 -$20.00
Plate 370. Singer ....$100.00 – $125.00	Plate 427. USSR $130.00
Plate 371. Singer ....$100.00 – $125.00	Plate 428. USSR $120.00
Plate 372. Singer ....$100.00 – $125.00	Plate 429. Vulcan............................$75.00 – $95.00
Plate 373. Singer ....$100.00 – $135.00	Plate 430. Vulcan............................$65.00 – $85.00
Plate 374. Singer ....$100.00 – $125.00	Plate 431. Vulcan............................$65.00 – $85.00
Plate 375. Singer ....$50.00 – $75.00	Plate 432. Vulcan............................$65.00 – $85.00

Plate 433. Vulcan.............................$75.00 – $95.00
Plate 434. Vulcan.............................$65.00 – $75.00
Plate 435. Vogue....................................NPA
Plate 436. Musical.................$100.00 – $150.00
Plate 437. Musical.................$100.00 – $150.00
Plate 438. Musical....................................NPA
Plate 439. Musical..............................$120.00
Plate 440. Musical..............................$200.00
Plate 441. Musical..............................$200.00
Plate 442. Musical....................................NPA
Plate 443. Musical....................................NPA
Plate 444. Musical................................$25.00
Plate 445. Musical................................$30.00
Plate 446. Musical................................$15.00
Plate 447. Musical................................$30.00
Plate 448. Musical................................$33.00
Plate 449. Musical................................$12.00
Plate 450. Musical................................$40.00
Plate 451. Musical................................$40.00
Plate 452. Musical................................$30.00
Plate 453. Musical................................$30.00
Plate 454. Treadle...................................NPA
Plate 455. Treadle...................................NPA
Plate 456. Treadle...................................NPA
Plate 457. Treadle...................................NPA
Plate 458. Treadle...................................NPA
Plate 459. Treadle...................................NPA
Plate 460. Treadle...................................NPA
Plate 461. Treadle...................................NPA
Plate 462. Treadle...................................NPA
Plate 463. Misc. $30.00
Plate 464. Misc....................................NPA
Plate 465. Misc. $4.00
Plate 466. Misc. $25.00
Plate 467. Misc. $8.00
Plate 468. Misc. $25.00
Plate 469. Misc. $3.00
Plate 470. Misc. $6.00
Plate 471. Misc. $6.00
Plate 472. Misc. ....$6.00 – $10.00
Plate 473. Misc. ....$6.00 – $10.00
Plate 474. Misc. $6.00
Plate 475. Misc. $4.00
Plate 476. Misc. $5.00
Plate 477. Misc. $3.00
Plate 478. Misc. $3.00
Plate 479. Misc. $3.00
Plate 480. Misc. $3.00
Plate 481. Misc. $3.00
Plate 482. Misc. $6.00
Plate 483. Misc. $2.00

Plate 484. Misc. $8.00
Plate 485. Misc. $2.00
Plate 486. Misc. $4.00
Plate 487. Misc. $2.00
Plate 488. Misc. ....NPA
Plate 489. Misc. ....NPA
Plate 490. Misc. $8.00
Plate 491. Misc. $17.00
Plate 492. Misc. $4.00
Plate 493. Misc. $3.00
Plate 494. Misc. $4.00
Plate 495. Misc. $5.00
Plate 496. Misc. $4.00
Plate 497. Misc. $5.00
Plate 498. Misc. $8.00
Plate 499. Misc. $8.00
Plate 500. Misc. $6.00
Plate 501. Misc. $11.00
Plate 502. Misc. $3.00
Plate 503. Misc. $8.00
Plate 504. Misc. $7.00
Plate 505. Misc. $4.00
Plate 506. Misc. $4.00
Plate 507. Misc. $4.00
Plate 508. Misc. ....$8.00 – $10.00
Plate 509. Misc. ....$8.00 – $10.00
Plate 510. Misc. ....$8.00 – $10.00
Plate 511. Misc. $6.00
Plate 512. Misc. $3.00
Plate 513. Misc. $6.00
Plate 514. Misc. $9.00
Plate 515. Misc. $6.00
Plate 516. Misc. $6.00
Plate 517. Misc. ....$8.00 – $10.00
Plate 518. Misc. ....$8.00 – $10.00
Plate 519. Misc. ....$5.00 – $8.00
Plate 520. Misc. ....$5.00 – $8.00
Plate 521. Misc. $65.00
Plate 522. Misc. $21.00
Plate 523. Misc. ....$10.00 – $15.00
Plate 524. Misc. ....$10.00 – $15.00
Plate 525. Misc. $4.00
Plate 526. Misc. ....$3.00 – $5.00
Plate 527. Misc. ....NPA
Plate 528. Misc. $10.00
Plate 529. Misc. ....NPA
Plate 530. Misc. $6.00
Plate 531. Misc. ....$3.00 – $5.00

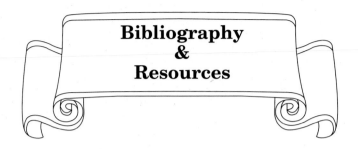

Bibliography & Resources

Current publication dedicated to toy sewing machines
Toy Stitchers Editor Claire Toschi
Semi-Monthly, $18.00 USA, Outside USA $24.00
623 Santa Florita, Millbrae, CA 94030
If you write and request a reply, please include SASE.

ISMACS NEWS- Publication about domestics and toy machines
Journal of the International Sewing Machine Collectors' Society
Maggie Snell, Editor; Graham Forsdyke, Research Editor
48 Nightingale House, Thomas More Street, London EI 9UB, England
Includes quarterly magazine (40 pages) and monthly meetings.
Subscriptions £13UK, £15 Europe, £18 ($35.00) USA.
USA contact is Sharron Tedrow, P.O. Box 336 Orcas, WA 09280 Tel. (206) 373-2829

* *

Asakawa, Gil & Leland Rucke
The Toy Book.
Alfred A. Knopf, Inc. 1991.

Baker, Linda.
Modern Toys–American Toys 1930-1980.
Paducah, Kentucky: Collector Books 1985.

Bays, Carter.
Encyclopedia of Early American Sewing Machines.
Columbia, SC 1993.

Brandon, Ruth.
A Capitalist Romance–Singer and the Sewing Machine.

Bridgeport Sunday Post: December 15, 1940, Bridgeport, Connecticut.

Benz, Bob.
The Purple Kangaroo, Original Roo.
Palmer Pletsch, Inc., 1987.

Clabburn, Pamela.
The Needleworker's Dictionary.
New York: William Morrow & Co., Inc.

Cleary, David Powers.
Great American Brands.

Clotilde, Inc.

Catalog of Sewing Notions for 22 years, includes many photos of antique sewing items.
1-800-772-2891
2 Sew Smart Way B8031
Stevens Point, WI 54481-8081

Cooper, Grace Rogers.
The Sewing Machine, Its Invention & Development.
Smithsonian Institution Press, 1976.

Davidson, Marshall B.
American Heritage History

Davis, Marvin & Helen.
Collector's Price Guide to Bottles, Tobacco Tins, and Relics.
New York: A & W Visual Library, 1974.

Desmonde, Kay.
A Color Book of Dolls,
London: Octopus Book
New York: Crescent Book ,1974.

Ewers, William, H.W., Baylor, H. H. Kenage.
Sincere's History of the Sewing Machine.
Sincere Press

Flick.
Discovering Toys and Toy Museums
UK: Shire Publications 1971.

Foley, Dan.
Toys Through The Ages 1962
Philadelphia and New York: Chilton Books, 1962.

Freeman, Ruth & Larry Freeman.
Cavalcade of Toys.
NY: Century House, 1942.

Gilbert, K. R.
Sewing Machines—A Science Museum Booklet.
Printed in England for Her Majesty's Stationary
Office.

Godfrey, Frank P.
An International History of the Sewing Machine.
London: Robert Hale Limited, 1982

Groves, Sylvia.
History of Needlework Tools & Accessories.
New York: Arco Publishing Co., Inc.

Hertz, Louis H.
The Handbook of Old American Toys.
Wethersfield, CT: Mark Haber Co., 1974

History of Bridgeport and Vicinity.
Volume II.
The S. J. Clarke Publishing Company., 1917

Jewell, Brian F.
Veteran Sewing Machines.
Cranbury, N J: A. S. Barnes & Co., Inc. 1975

Jewell, Brian F.
Antique Sewing Machines.
England: O. J. Costello Ltd., 1985.

Johnson-Shrebro, Nancy.
Featherweight 221, The Perfect Portable.
Tunkhannock, PA: Silver Star Publishing, 1992.

Kovel, Ralph & Terry.
Know Your Antiques.
New York: Crown Publishers, Inc., 1967.

King, Constance.
Antique Toys and Dolls.
Rizzoli International Publications Inc., 1979.

King Constance
The Encyclopedia of Toys.
Secaucus, N J: Chartwell Books, 1978.

Landgraf, Otto.
Oldtimer Sewing Machines.
Germany: Wepert GmbH & Co. KG

Longest, David.
Toys -Antique & Collectible
Paducah, Kentucky: Collector Books.

Matter, Darryl & Roxana.
Collector's Guide to Toy Sewing Machines.
Lima, Ohio: Golden Ea Publications, 1991

McClintock, Inez & Marshall.
Toys in America.
Washington, DC: Public Affairs Press, 1961

McClinton, Katherine.
Antiques—An Encyclopedia of the Decorative Arts.
Octopus Books Limited,
Produced by Mandarin Publications, 1979.

Orcutt, Rev. Samuel.
History of City of Bridgeport.
Fairfield County Historical Society.

Pinsky, Maxine A.
Greenberg's Guide to Marx Toys, Volume I.
Sykesville, MD: Greenberg Publishing Co., Inc. 1988.

Powell, Anne. LTd.
A Catalog of Fine Needlework Supplies & Gifts.
P. O. Box 3060
Stuart, Florida 34995 - 3060
Catalog $5.00

Revi, Albert Christian.
The Spinning Wheel's Complete Book of Antiques.
New York: Grosset & Dunlap Publishers, 1978

Schroeder, Joseph J. Jr.
The Wonderful World of Toys, Games, and Dolls.
Northfield, Il: DBI Books.

Sew News Magazine
P. O. Box 3138
Harlan, IA 51593
Twelve issues $21.98 (USA) Articles about sewing col-
lectables and sources for all sewing supplies. May 1992
Issue: *Toy Treasures* by Marjorie Abel and Gail Brown.

Sommer, Robin Langley.
I Had One of Those Toys
Brompton Books Corp. 1992.

Toy Collector Magazine, 1992 & 1993 Issues have toy
sewing machine articles by Marc Horovitz.
Subscription Dept.
P. O. Box 550
Mt. Morris, IL 61054

University of Reading
Sewing Machines A Catalog of the Barnett Collection.
England.

Whiting, Gertrude.
Old Time Tools & Toys of Needlework.
Dover Publications, 1971.

Wilhelm, Peter.
Old French Sewing Machines.

Wilhelm, Peter.
Alte deutsche Nähmaschinen.
Germany: Marke Druck & Verlag.

Wilhelm, Peter,
F. W. Müller's Toy Sewing Machines.
Germany: Mecke Druck & Verlag, 1988.

Wilhelm, Peter.
Geman Toy Sewing Machines.
Bergstrasse La, D37130
Gleichen, Germany

Zalkin, Estelle.
Zalkin's Handbook of Thimbles & Sewing Implements.
Chilton Book Co.

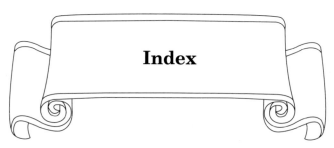

Index

Books on Antiques and Collectibles

This is only a partial listing of the books on antiques that are available from Collector Books. All books are well illustrated and contain current values. Most of the following books are available from your local book seller, antique dealer, or public library. If you are unable to locate certain titles in your area, you may order by mail from COLLECTOR BOOKS, P.O. Box 3009, Paducah, KY 42002-3009. Customers with Visa or MasterCard may phone in orders from 8:00 – 4:00 CST, M – F – Toll Free 1-800-626-5420. Add $2.00 for postage for the first book ordered and $0.30 for each additional book. Include item number, title, and price when ordering. Allow 14 to 21 days for delivery.

BOOKS ON GLASS AND POTTERY

1810	American Art Glass, Shuman	$29.95
1312	Blue & White Stoneware, McNerney	$9.95
1959	Blue Willow, 2nd Ed., Gaston	$14.95
3719	Coll. Glassware from the 40's, 50's, 60's, 2nd Ed., Florence	$19.95
3816	Collectible Vernon Kilns, Nelson	$24.95
3311	Collecting Yellow Ware – Id. & Value Gd., McAllister	$16.95
1373	Collector's Ency. of American Dinnerware, Cunningham	$24.95
3815	Coll. Ency. of Blue Ridge Dinnerware, Newbound	$19.95
2272	Collector's Ency. of California Pottery, Chipman	$24.95
3811	Collector's Ency. of Colorado Pottery, Carlton	$24.95
3312	Collector's Ency. of Children's Dishes, Whitmyer	$19.95
2133	Collector's Ency. of Cookie Jars, Roerig	$24.95
3723	Coll. Ency. of Cookie Jars-Volume II, Roerig	$24.95
3724	Collector's Ency. of Depression Glass, 11th Ed., Florence	$19.95
2209	Collector's Ency. of Fiesta, 7th Ed., Huxford	$19.95
1439	Collector's Ency. of Flow Blue China, Gaston	$19.95
3812	Coll. Ency. of Flow Blue China, 2nd Ed., Gaston	$24.95
3813	Collector's Ency. of Hall China, 2nd Ed., Whitmyer	$24.95
2334	Collector's Ency. of Majolica Pottery, Katz-Marks	$19.95
1358	Collector's Ency. of McCoy Pottery, Huxford	$19.95
3313	Collector's Ency. of Niloak, Gifford	$19.95
3837	Collector's Ency. of Nippon Porcelain I, Van Patten	$24.95
2089	Collector's Ency. of Nippon Porcelain II, Van Patten	$24.95
1665	Collector's Ency. of Nippon Porcelain III, Van Patten	$24.95
1447	Collector's Ency. of Noritake, 1st Series, Van Patten	$19.95
1034	Collector's Ency. of Roseville Pottery, Huxford	$19.95
1035	Collector's Ency. of Roseville Pottery, 2nd Ed., Huxford	$19.95
3314	Collector's Ency. of Van Briggle Art Pottery, Sasicki	$24.95
3433	Collector's Guide To Harker Pottery - U.S.A., Colbert	$17.95
2339	Collector's Guide to Shawnee Pottery, Vanderbilt	$19.95
1425	Cookie Jars, Westfall	$9.95
3440	Cookie Jars, Book II, Westfall	$19.95
2275	Czechoslovakian Glass & Collectibles, Barta	$16.95
3882	Elegant Glassware of the Depression Era, 6th Ed., Florence	$19.95
3725	Fostoria - Pressed, Blown & Hand Molded Shapes, Kerr	$24.95
3883	Fostoria Stemware - The Crystal for America, Long	$24.95
3886	Kitchen Glassware of the Depression Years, 5th Ed., Florence	$19.95
3889	Pocket Guide to Depression Glass, 9th Ed., Florence	$9.95
3825	Puritan Pottery, Morris	$24.95
1670	Red Wing Collectibles, DePasquale	$9.95
1440	Red Wing Stoneware, DePasquale	$9.95
1958	So. Potteries Blue Ridge Dinnerware, 3rd Ed., Newbound	$14.95
3739	Standard Carnival Glass, 4th Ed., Edwards	$24.95
3327	Watt Pottery – Identification & Value Guide, Morris	$19.95
2224	World of Salt Shakers, 2nd Ed., Lechner	$24.95

BOOKS ON DOLLS & TOYS

2079	Barbie Fashion, Vol. 1, 1959-1967, Eames	$24.95
3310	Black Dolls – 1820 - 1991 - Id. & Value Guide, Perkins	$17.95
3810	Chatty Cathy Dolls, Lewis	$15.95
1529	Collector's Ency. of Barbie Dolls, DeWein	$19.95
2338	Collector's Ency. of Disneyana, Longest & Stern	$24.95
3727	Coll. Guide to Ideal Dolls, Izen	$18.95
3822	Madame Alexander Price Guide #19, Smith	$9.95
3732	Matchbox Toys, 1948 to 1993, Johnson	$18.95

3733	Modern Collector's Dolls, 6th series, Smith	$24.95
1540	Modern Toys, 1930 - 1980, Baker	$19.95
3824	Patricia Smith's Doll Values – Antique to Modern, 10th ed	$12.95
3826	Story of Barbie, Westenhouser, No Values	$19.95
2028	Toys, Antique & Collectible, Longest	$14.95
1808	Wonder of Barbie, Manos	$9.95
1430	World of Barbie Dolls, Manos	$9.95

OTHER COLLECTIBLES

1457	American Oak Furniture, McNerney	$9.95
3716	American Oak Furniture, Book II, McNerney	$12.95
2333	Antique & Collectible Marbles, 3rd Ed., Grist	$9.95
1748	Antique Purses, Holiner	$19.95
1426	Arrowheads & Projectile Points, Hothem	$7.95
1278	Art Nouveau & Art Deco Jewelry, Baker	$9.95
1714	Black Collectibles, Gibbs	$19.95
1128	Bottle Pricing Guide, 3rd Ed., Cleveland	$7.95
3717	Christmas Collectibles, 2nd Ed., Whitmyer	$24.95
1752	Christmas Ornaments, Johnston	$19.95
3718	Collectible Aluminum, Grist	$16.95
2132	Collector's Ency. of American Furniture, Vol. I, Swedberg	$24.95
2271	Collector's Ency. of American Furniture, Vol. II, Swedberg	$24.95
3720	Coll. Ency. of American Furniture, Vol III, Swedberg	$24.95
3722	Coll. Ency. of Compacts, Carryalls & Face Powder Boxes, Mueller	$24.95
2018	Collector's Ency. of Granite Ware, Greguire	$24.95
3430	Coll. Ency. of Granite Ware, Book 2, Greguire	$24.95
1441	Collector's Guide to Post Cards, Wood	$9.95
2276	Decoys, Kangas	$24.95
1629	Doorstops – Id. & Values, Bertoia	$9.95
1716	Fifty Years of Fashion Jewelry, Baker	$19.95
3817	Flea Market Trader, 9th Ed., Huxford	$12.95
3731	Florence's Standard Baseball Card Price Gd., 6th Ed.	$9.95
3819	General Store Collectibles, Wilson	$24.95
3436	Grist's Big Book of Marbles, Everett Grist	$19.95
2278	Grist's Machine Made & Contemporary Marbles	$9.95
1424	Hatpins & Hatpin Holders, Baker	$9.95
3884	Huxford's Collectible Advertising – Id. & Value Gd., 2nd Ed	$24.95
3820	Huxford's Old Book Value Guide, 6th Ed.	$19.95
3821	Huxford's Paperback Value Guide	$19.95
1181	100 Years of Collectible Jewelry, Baker	$9.95
2216	Kitchen Antiques – 1790 - 1940, McNerney	$14.95
3887	Modern Guns – Id. & Val. Gd., 10th Ed., Quertermous	$12.95
3734	Pocket Guide to Handguns, Quertermous	$9.95
3735	Pocket Guide to Rifles, Quertermous	$9.95
3736	Pocket Guide to Shotguns, Quertermous	$9.95
2026	Railroad Collectibles, 4th Ed., Baker	$14.95
1632	Salt & Pepper Shakers, Guarnaccia	$9.95
1888	Salt & Pepper Shakers II, Guarnaccia	$14.95
2220	Salt & Pepper Shakers III, Guarnaccia	$14.95
3443	Salt & Pepper Shakers IV, Guarnaccia	$18.95
3890	Schroeder's Antiques Price Guide, 13th Ed.	$12.95
2096	Silverplated Flatware, 4th Ed., Hagan	$14.95
2348	20th Century Fashionable Plastic Jewelry, Baker	$19.95
3828	Value Guide to Advertising Memorabilia, Summers	$18.95
3830	Vintage Vanity Bags & Purses, Gerson	$24.95

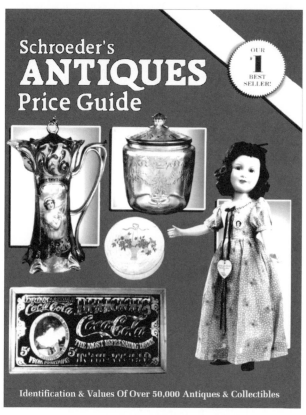